P9-CKN-890
GRAND CANYON ASSOCIATION

POST OFFICE BOX 399
GRAND CANYON, AZ 86023
520-638-2481
www.grandcanyon.org

ISBN 0-938216-75-9
Library of Congress Control Number: 00-136067
First Edition

10 9 8 7 6 5 4 3 2 1

PROJECT MANAGER: Pam Frazier
EDITORIAL: Greer Price and Faith Marcovecchio
BOOK DESIGN: Carol Haralson
MAPS: Bangfish Productions
Printed in China

Grand Canyon Association is a non-profit organization whose mission is *to cultivate knowledge, discovery, and stewardship* for the benefit of Grand Canyon National Park and its visitors. Proceeds from the sale of this book will be used to support the educational goals of Grand Canyon National Park.

Preceding page: Cedar Mountain from Desert View
Front cover: View from Mather Point
Back cover: View to the east at sunset from Desert View Drive

ACKNOWLEDGMENTS

A visitors' guide to specific scenic and historic points on the South Rim posed special concerns for organization and design. Grand Canyon Association staff and their contractors were, as usual, equal to the task. Pam Frazier, L. Greer Price, Faith Marcovecchio, and designer Carol Haralson accepted the disparate parts I contributed and transformed them into something beautiful and comprehensible, no mean feat given my artistic limitations. I am especially grateful to Gary Ladd, one of the finest landscape photographers in the Southwest, for adding color, wonder, and insight to these pages; and to Don Keil for providing access to unusual vantage points. Thanks to those at the park's research library and museum collection who abided my presence and questions: Sara Stebbins, Mike Quinn, Colleen Hyde, Carolyn Richard, Kim Besom, and Alice Ponyah.

Much of the park was first developed by the park's concessioner, the Fred Harvey Company. Fred Harvey, celebrating its 100th anniversary at Grand Canyon in 2000, merged with AmFac, Inc. in 1968 and continues to offer accommodations, meals, and other services to park visitors. I thank Bill Johnston, general manager of South Rim operations, for his support on this project. I am also very grateful to Dennis Reason, the concessioner's education specialist and a good friend, for the historical information and thoughtful comments gladly contributed.

M.F. ANDERSON

CONTENTS

INTRODUCTION 7

GRAND CANYON VILLAGE 10

walking tour, dining and hotels, historic buildings

1 Mather Point / Canyon View Information Plaza 14
2 Yavapai Point 16
3 Santa Fe Railroad Depot 18
4 El Tovar Hotel 20
5 Bright Angel Lodge 24
6 Lookout Studio 26
7 Kolb Studio 28
8 Maswik Lodge and Vicinity 30
9 Mule Barns and Vicinity 32

HERMIT ROAD [WEST RIM] 34

great views of the river

10 Trailview Overlooks 38
11 Maricopa Point 40
12 Powell Point and Memorial 42
13 Hopi Point 44
14 Mohave Point 46
15 Pima Point 48
16 Hermits Rest 50

DESERT VIEW DRIVE [EAST RIM] 52

panoramas and the watchtower

17 Yaki Point 56
18 Grandview Point 58
19 Moran Point 60
20 Tusayan Ruin 62
21 Lipan Point 64
22 Desert View 66

Nature Along the Rim 70

MAPS

SOUTH RIM 4-5
VILLAGE 12-13
HERMIT ROAD 36-37
DESERT VIEW DRIVE 54-55

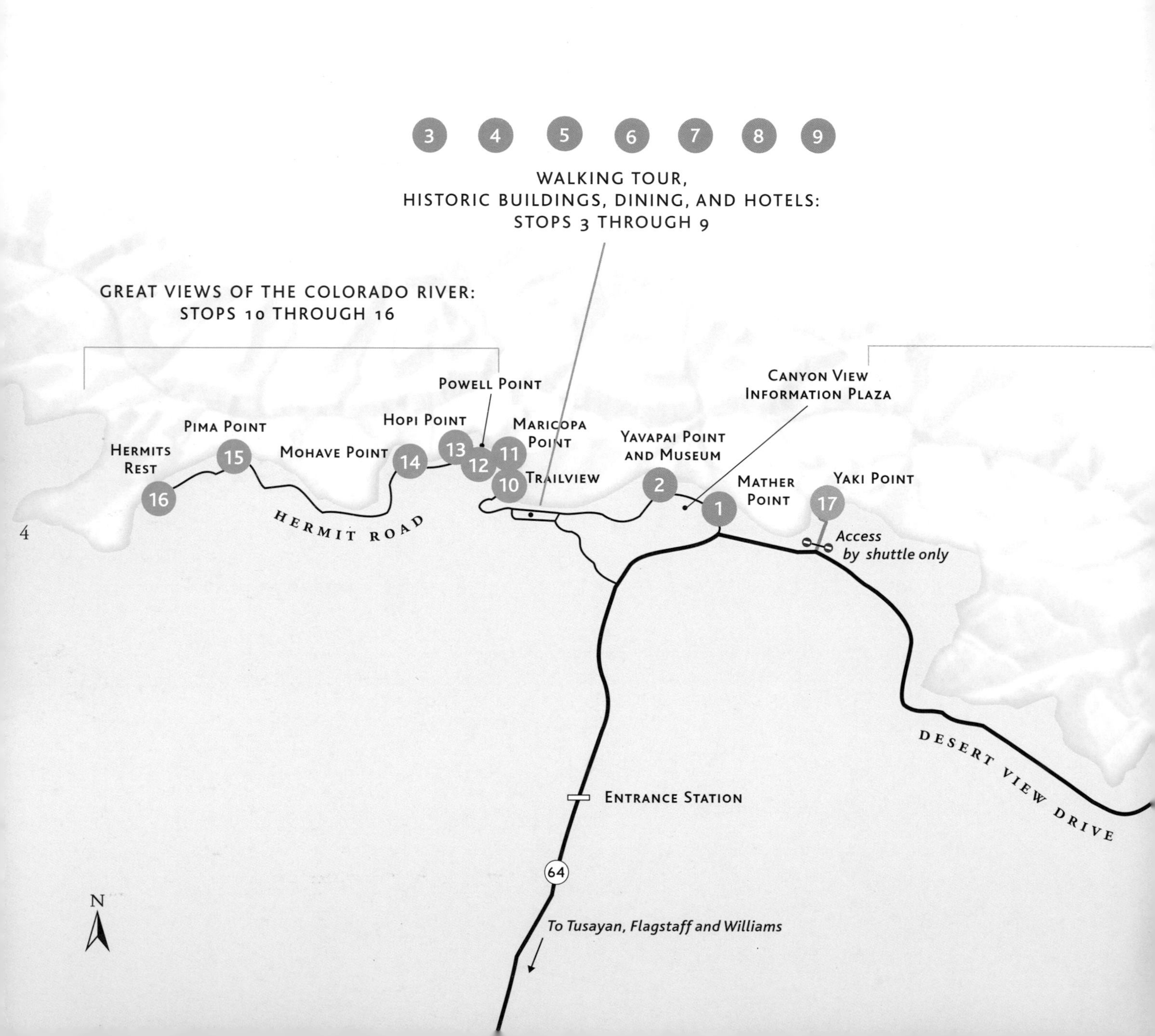
3
4
5
6
7
8
9
WALKING TOUR,
HISTORIC BUILDINGS, DINING, AND HOTELS:
STOPS 3 THROUGH 9
GREAT VIEWS OF THE COLORADO RIVER:
STOPS 10 THROUGH 16
Powell Point
Canyon View
Information Plaza
Pima Point
Hopi Point
Maricopa
Point
Yavapai Point
and Museum
Hermits
Rest
Mohave Point
Trailview
Mather
Point
Yaki Point
15
14
13
12
11
10
2
1
17
16
Hermit Road
Access
by shuttle only
Desert View Drive
Entrance Station
64
N
To Tusayan, Flagstaff and Williams

PANORAMIC VIEWS AND THE WATCHTOWER: STOPS 17 THROUGH 22

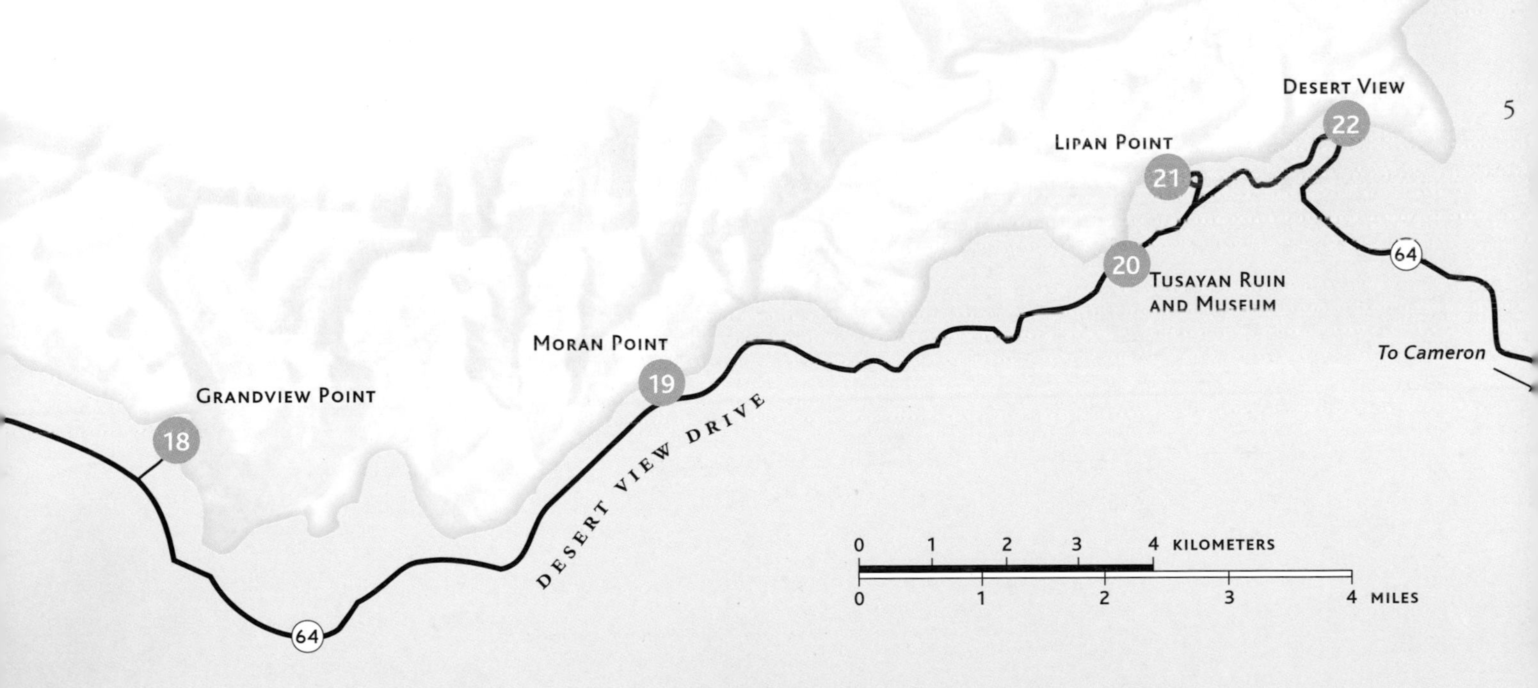

Mather Point

"IT IS ALL BEETHOVEN'S NINE SYMPHONIES IN STONE AND MAGIC LIGHT. EVEN TO REMEMBER THAT IT IS STILL THERE LIFTS UP THE HEART."

— *J. B. Priestly*

"IT SEEMS A GIGANTIC STATEMENT FOR EVEN NATURE TO MAKE. . . ."

— *John Muir*

GRAND CANYON National Park offers its visitors fascinating human history as well as unmatched scenic views. Ancient American Indian peoples roamed the region for ten thousand years before modern tribes began to settle nearly a millennium ago. European American trappers, explorers, surveyors, and settlers followed, most coming after the United States wrested the land from Mexico in 1848 and from native residents in the decades that followed. The canyon remained unassigned public domain until President Benjamin Harrison proclaimed it a national forest reserve in 1893. Succeeding designations as game preserve (1906), national monument (1908), and national park (1919) recognized the need to protect the canyon's unique ecosystems and to develop small areas to accommodate the visiting public.

Since the 1870s visitors have flocked to the South Rim on foot and horseback, in wagons and stagecoaches, by rail, automobiles, and buses, and more recently by air. Travel along the rim has also evolved—from foot, horse, and buggy to automobiles, bicycles, and shuttle buses. How you get here and maneuver within the park is immaterial to this guide. This book is organized in three sections with maps that will allow you to find your way to points of interest, regardless of your mode of travel. Shuttle buses serve portions of the South Rim; check the park newspaper, *The Guide,* for information during your stay. Much of historic Grand Canyon Village is best seen on foot. The Rim Trail from Hermits Rest to Grand Canyon Village, paralleling Hermit Road and accessible at many different points, offers extraordinary views of the canyon.

Each of the three sections of this book is prefaced with a few opening remarks, providing background to the history and development of that portion of the South Rim. At the end of the book you'll find a suggested reading list. Many of the items listed there are available in stores in the park and will allow you to learn more about individual stories.

The developed South Rim extends from Hermits Rest on the west to Desert View on the east, a distance of about thirty-five miles, with elevations ranging from 6,600 feet to 7,500 feet. Most points are on the rim, and you may find yourself overwhelmed by the

Grand Canyon National Park was established in 1919, only three years after the creation of the National Park Service. President Woodrow Wilson used the pen below to sign the enabling legislation.

The Colorado River—lifeline of the canyon—lies nearly a vertical mile beneath the South Rim and is visible only from certain viewpoints. While small stretches of the river (as well as Phantom Ranch) are visible from Yavapai Point, the most expansive views are from overlooks on Hermit Road (Hopi, Mohave, and Pima) and from Desert View, at the far east end of Desert View Drive.

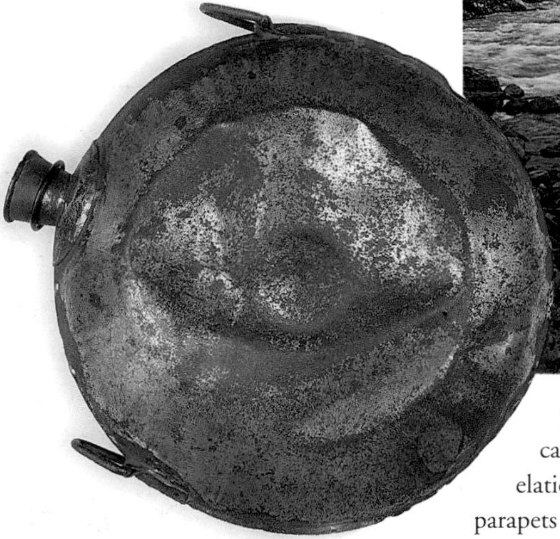

yawning abyss. First glimpses can cause nausea or vertigo, tears or laughter, elation or depression, so stay within stone parapets and metal railings where they exist. After the shock wears off, appreciate the canyon for what it is: a glimpse of geologic history in a landscape shaped by wind and water, freeze, thaw, and gravity, laid bare for thoughtful examination.

The North Rim on the far side of the canyon is roughly ten miles away as the raven flies, more than twenty miles on foot via inner-canyon trails, and a thousand feet higher than the South Rim. The Colorado River is nearly a vertical mile below. The gnarled metamorphic rock rising from the river was formed nearly two billion years ago. The soft green tableland visible from most points is the Tonto Platform, a broad erosional bench formed in the Bright Angel Shale. Several thousand feet of sandstone, limestone, and shale lie between the Tonto Platform and the Kaibab Limestone on the rim. Now imagine another vertical mile of sedimentary rock above your head, long since eroded away, and the immensity of geologic time becomes a bit more comprehensible.

Amble a few hundred yards to either side of scenic overlooks for more intimate views, silence, and a chance to glimpse the rim's marvelous diversity of plants and wildlife. Most paths lead through pinyon pine and Utah juniper, often windblown into exotic shapes; they provide pleasing foregrounds to canyon photographs. Scrub and Gambel oaks, cliffrose, sage, and several species of cactus conceal ground squirrels and field mice, prey for the occasional hawk and peregrine falcon. Raucous ravens glide among violet-green swallows and white-throated swifts darting among the cliffs below. You will never be far from magnificent stands of ponderosa pine that hide goshawks and tassel-eared Abert squirrels. Mule deer are common, and with a fair measure of luck you may spot an elk, coyote, bobcat, or mountain lion among the trees, a golden eagle or California condor touching the sky. Venture a quarter mile or more down inner-canyon trails from Hermits Rest, Kolb Studio, Yaki, Grandview, and Lipan Points for entirely new perspectives. And take your time; the canyon has.

Indian paintbrush (*Castilleja linariaefolia*), a harbinger of spring in the woodlands of the South Rim, provides a welcome splash of color and blooms throughout the summer. Below: Fog enshrouds the rim at Yaki Point.

Below: Lookout Studio, 1920.
At right: View of the South Rim, circa 1974. Kolb Studio sits precariously on the canyon rim in the foreground.

Grand Canyon Village owes its existence to pioneer prospectors, tourism operators, and promoters. Prospectors Pete Berry and Ralph Cameron built the Bright Angel Trail in 1890-91, and Flagstaff businessman James Thurber erected the Bright Angel Hotel near the trailhead in 1896, but an ebullient young man named William "Buckey" O'Neill proved the key element. Buckey was a frontier jack-of-all-trades who seemingly never slept. A lawyer, newspaperman, sheriff, author, miner, and mayor of Prescott, Arizona, he still found time to roam the canyon, befriend its denizens, and build a cabin beside Thurber's hotel. When, in 1897, he helped organize a railroad to reach the South Rim, it was only natural to survey the rail spur directly north from the Santa Fe Railroad's transcontinental line at Williams to O'Neill's cabin beside the rim.

Mining efforts waned, Buckey died in the Spanish-American War, and his railroad went bust ten miles short of the canyon, but Santa Fe Railroad officials recognized a good thing. They bought up the failed company, renamed it the Grand Canyon Railway, and finished laying track in September 1901. In the following year they platted a twenty-acre depot site east of the Bright Angel trailhead, which, along with their two-hundred-foot right-of-way along the rails, represented the only valid land claims in Grand Canyon Village. Railroad depots formed the nuclei of frontier towns across America in the nineteenth and early twentieth centuries; Grand Canyon Village was no exception.

For the following half century, Santa Fe Railroad officials built nearly all of the village's hotels, restaurants, curio shops, rest stops, lookouts, and public utilities. During 1901-19 they and their partner, the Fred Harvey Company,

Left: Victor Hall Annex, one of the Fred Harvey dormitories, on its way to its new home on the other side of Grand Canyon Village. The building was moved in 1938 to its present location. Below: Aerial view of Grand Canyon Village, circa 1935. The Bright Angel tent camp is visible at the center of the photo.

THE ATCHESON, TOPEKA & SANTA FE RAILROAD

Beginning in 1872, and for a century thereafter, railroads played a crucial role in creating, developing, and marketing the western national parks. The Santa Fe's role at Grand Canyon began when it finished laying track across northern Arizona in 1881-83, bringing transcontinental travelers within sixty-five miles of the South Rim. The railway's relationship with the canyon grew more intimate in 1901 when it completed a spur from its main line at Williams, Arizona, inaugurating development of today's Grand Canyon Village.

The Santa Fe's partnership with the Fred Harvey Company began in 1876 when Harvey, an enterprising English immigrant, offered to manage Santa Fe eating establishments ("Harvey Houses") alongside its rails. Passengers and railroad officials were very pleased with quality service at reasonable prices and with Harvey's well-trained, attractive waitresses ("Harvey Girls"); there was never any doubt who would run the South Rim hotels and restaurants.

This symbiotic partnership, forged with the proverbial handshake, flourished at Grand Canyon from 1905 until 1954. Railroad officials along with the U.S. Forest Service (1905-19) then National Park Service determined the location, extent, and architecture of visitor facilities. The Santa Fe built and paid for them and Fred Harvey managed them to most everyone's satisfaction.

Many were saddened in 1954 when Santa Fe managers, for financial reasons, donated utility-related buildings and structures to the National Park Service and sold their tourism-related properties to the Fred Harvey Company at bargain basement prices. The railroad continued passenger service until 1968, and freight service for a few years longer, before bowing out of the canyon entirely in 1972.

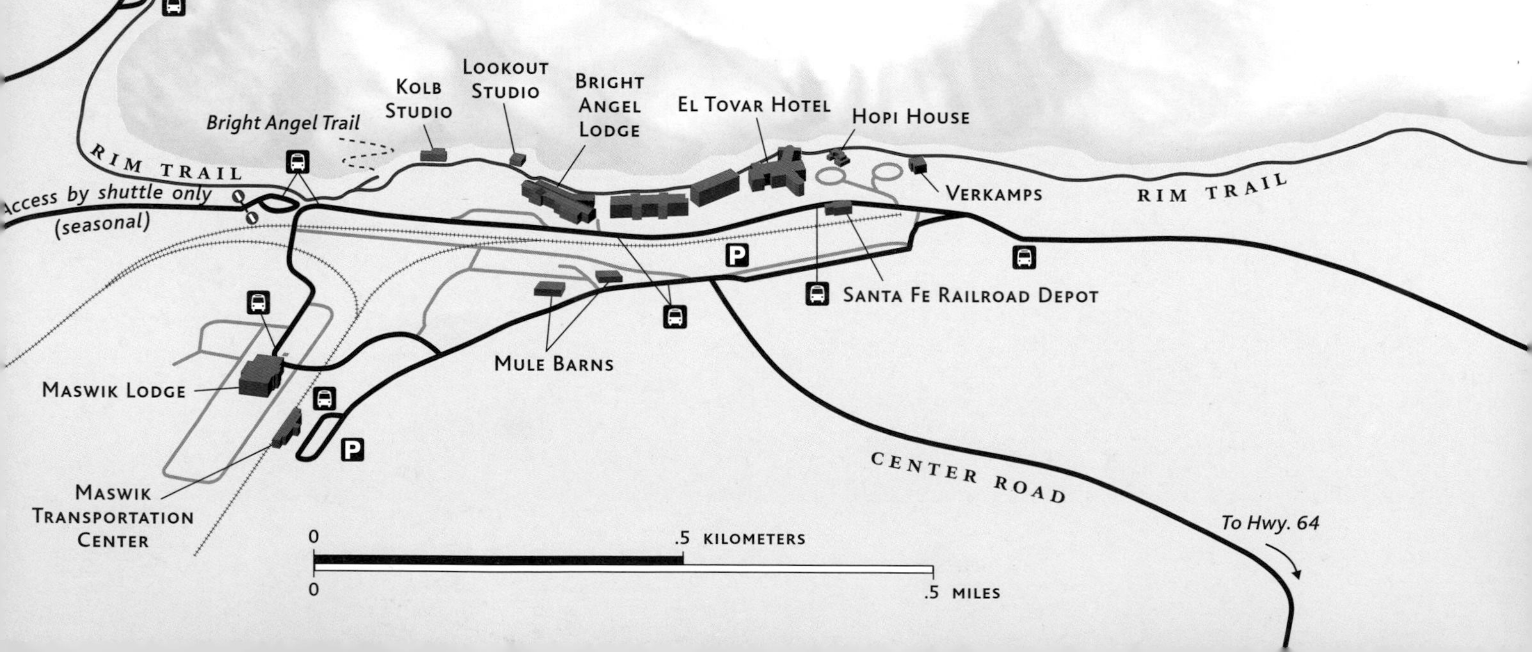

determined what would be built and where, reserving the rim for tourist amenities while relegating most support structures to areas along the tracks within Bright Angel Wash. From 1919 until the onset of World War II, the National Park Service gained control of the developing landscape by enforcing a village blueprint of administrative, accommodation, industrial, and residential zones. Most buildings in the village historic district derive from these two periods.

The historic village is perhaps best appreciated by beginning—as the village began—at the head of the Bright Angel Trail. Many visitors a century ago started in the same place, ambling east atop a boardwalk behind a rail fence, pausing at Kolb Studio, The Lookout, Bright Angel Lodge, and El Tovar Hotel. But since 1953, with the completion of the new south entrance road, Mather Point has been the first canyon viewpoint most visitors encounter approaching the park from the south.

NOTE: *Check the park newspaper,* THE GUIDE, *for shuttle schedules and other useful information.*

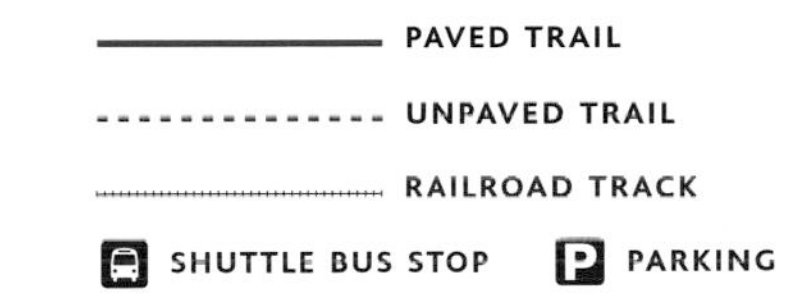

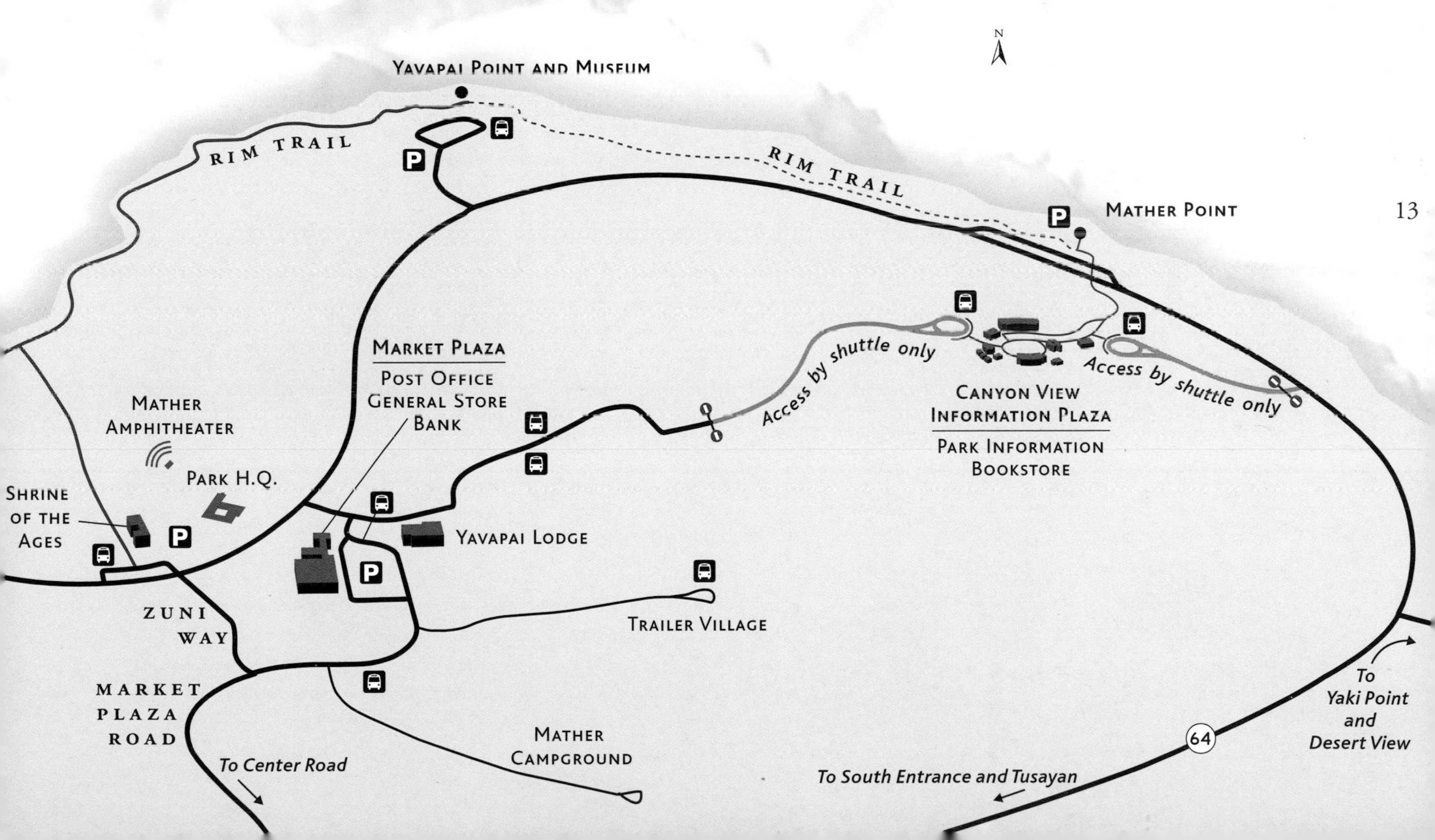

MATHER POINT/CANYON VIEW INFORMATION PLAZA

THE *most visited point* ON EITHER RIM, MATHER POINT IS NAMED FOR THE FIRST NATIONAL PARK SERVICE DIRECTOR.

Stephen Mather was an idealist and consummate salesman. His invaluable assistant, Horace Albright, was a pragmatist and natural-born politician. In every practical sense, the pair (though not legislators) created the National Park Service: outlining its mission, defining its goals, hiring professional managers, selling the park idea to Congress, businesses, and the public, expanding the park system, and protecting it from the worst effects of western exploitation. Both supervised the final stages of the thirty-seven-year fight to grant Grand Canyon the protection that finally brought it into the National Park System in 1919.

MATHER POINT is named for Stephen Tyng Mather, first director of the National Park Service. A retired millionaire with an uncommon devotion to fast automobiles and monumental western landscapes, in 1914 he complained to Interior Secretary Franklin Lane about the management of Yosemite and Sequoia National Parks. Lane wrote back: "... if you don't like the way the national parks are being run, come on down to Washington and run them yourself." Mather accepted the challenge, helped lead the struggle to create the National Park Service, and became its first director in 1916. His battles to protect public lands proved intense, and to a great degree led to Mather's long bouts of illness and untimely death shortly after his retirement from the National Park Service in 1929.

The panorama from Mather Point is somewhat restricted by Yavapai and Yaki Points, to the west and east respectively, but there is still much to see from its viewing platforms and adjacent paths. The broad Tonto Platform several thousand feet below forms the foreground, and an alert eye can pick out the faint path of the Tonto Trail, running roughly east-west but paralleling the edge of the Inner Gorge. Mather Point is also the best vantage from which to observe the South Kaibab Trail, tumbling from the rim beside Yaki Point, past O'Neill Butte, on its way to the Colorado River.

The tiny green oasis across the river near the mouth of Bright Angel Canyon is Phantom Ranch, a site first developed in 1906 by North Rim entrepreneurs Edwin Dilworth "Uncle Dee" Woolley and his son-in-law, David Rust. Some of the willows and cottonwoods planted by Rust still shade the spot, but his camp was replaced in 1922 with the present rustic resort, designed by Mary Colter for the Santa Fe Railroad. The Civilian Conservation Corps maintained a work camp below the ranch in the 1930s (today's Bright Angel Campground), and the spot remains a strategic stopover for river runners and backpackers.

ISIS TEMPLE
NORTH RIM
INNER GORGE
PLATEAU POINT
COLORADO RIVER

2 YAVAPAI POINT

THE SOUTH RIM'S FIRST INTERPRETIVE CENTER—DATING TO 1928—AND *a place to see the canyon from indoors.*

Above: Ranger explaining Grand Canyon geology at Yavapai Observation Station, 1932. Below: Visitors at Yavapai Point in 1906, long before Yavapai Observation Station was built.

YAVAPAI OBSERVATION STATION, the South Rim's first museum and interpretive center, served in that capacity from its completion in 1928 until 1957. Today it houses a bookstore and exhibits and offers sheltered views of the canyon throughout the year. Prior to 1953 the station's north side, at the canyon's very edge, was open to the elements. Visitors spent hours along a low parapet lined with interpretive signs, viewfinders, binoculars, and a high-powered telescope.

The views, then as now, are stunning. Before construction of the road from Cameron in 1935 and a new entrance road from Williams in 1954, virtually all South Rim visitors arrived first at the village, where up- and downriver vistas are partially obstructed by Maricopa and Grandeur Points. Yavapai Point to the east, jutting into the canyon like a bulbous finger, offered the first panorama divulging the canyon's true shape, depth, width, and length.

A sideways glance reveals tributary canyons extending south and upward from the Colorado River, inner-canyon mesas that rise to projecting points, and recessed bays that almost touch the shoulders of Desert View Drive. In the distance upriver, Wotans Throne and Vishnu Temple emerge from the depths to brush the horizon beside North Rim's Cape Royal. The Palisades of the Desert, the line of cliffs that forms the east wall of the canyon beyond Desert View, bend north to meet the Little Colorado River. The view at

sunrise appears smoky and mysterious; near day's end it is an artist's pastel palette.

The paved path west of Yavapai affords partial glimpses of two historic inner-canyon camps. Lush foliage on the Tonto Platform beside the Bright Angel Trail denotes Indian Garden, developed around 1900 as a tent camp (where one could buy a cold beer for a nickel). Century-old cottonwoods and fresh water still make it a favored stop for hikers. A similar patch of green across the Colorado River near the mouth of Bright Angel Canyon marks Phantom Ranch, a rustic inner-canyon resort laid out by Mary Colter and built by the Santa Fe Railroad in 1922.

Although designed by the National Park Service in NPS Rustic style, Yavapai Observation Station (at right, in 1929) closely resembles Hermits Rest at the end of Hermit Road and Lookout Studio in the village, both designed by Santa Fe Railroad architect Mary Colter. Low walls, flat roofs, and rough-cut stone elements make the structure seem more an extension of the Kaibab Limestone than an artifact of man.

The tiny black line crossing the Colorado a bit upstream of Phantom Ranch is the 440-foot-long, 5-foot-wide Kaibab Suspension Bridge, built in 1928 to connect the South and North Kaibab Trails. National Park Service mules (at right) lugged nearly all of the 122 tons of materials needed for construction, but one-ton suspension cables were draped over the shoulders of forty-two men, mostly Havasupai laborers, who walked single file down the trail, appearing as a 550-foot-long snake to onlookers from the rim.

PHOTO BY MIKE BUCHHEIT

SANTA FE RAILROAD DEPOT

The only **RAIL STATION IN A NATIONAL PARK AND THE LAST SURVIVING DEPOT IN THE UNITED STATES THAT IS BUILT PRIMARILY OF LOGS.**

IN 1909 the Santa Fe Railroad commissioned Santa Barbara architect Francis Wilson to design a rail depot immediately below El Tovar Hotel and Hopi House. Wilson, who had earlier designed stations along the railroad's main line in Williams and Ash Fork, Arizona, and in Needles and Barstow, California, fashioned a rambling rustic structure to complement El Tovar Hotel. Completed in 1910, it is the only rail station in a national park and the only surviving depot in the United States built primarily of logs.

The federal government has managed South Rim activities since 1893, but the railroad dictated development, and the Fred Harvey Company supplied visitor information from its concession facilities until 1921. In that year the National Park Service (NPS) began to control building projects when its chief landscape engineer, Daniel Hull, completed a preliminary village development plan and, with the assistance of park superintendent Dewitt Reaburn, designed the park's first administration building. This lovely structure, at the foot of the hill

The Santa Fe Railroad depot today (above) looks much as it did when it was built in 1910. Right: The train and station crew pose before engine #1251 in 1915.

When the Santa Fe Railroad depot at Grand Canyon opened for business in 1910 (at right), the canyon was already a major destination for railroad travelers. Today thousands of people find their way to the canyon each year by train from Williams, thanks to service resumed in 1989 by Grand Canyon Railway.

below El Tovar, is the park's earliest example of NPS Rustic architecture. It functioned as an administrative center until 1929 and was remodeled as the superintendent's residence in 1931. Today it serves as offices for AmFac Parks and Resorts.

In 1914 the railroad added the Fred Harvey Garage to facilitate the transition from scenic buggy rides to motor tours and to accommodate the increasing numbers of tourists who arrived in their own automobiles. The garage, strategically placed at the intersection of early approach roads from Williams and Grandview, reflects one of several varieties of masonry construction found in the village today. Until 1938 it sported two gravity-fed gas pumps fronting Village Loop Drive.

The Fred Harvey Garage marks the easternmost boundary of the pre-park village. Gazing west, you can see the railroad tracks running down the bottom of Bright Angel Wash for half a mile (parallel with the canyon rim) before they turn south toward Williams. The shallow drainage suggested natural boundaries between tourist accommodations ranging up the north slope to the canyon rim, service structures along the bottom of the wash, and residences and administrative buildings on the gentler south slope, screened somewhat by ponderosa pines.

The north side of Village Loop Drive leads to Bright Angel Lodge, Kolb Studio, and the beginning of Hermit Road. (If you're on foot, the paved path along the rim offers a scenic alternative.)

Along Village Loop Drive on the right you will pass Colter Hall (below), built in 1937 as a fifty-two-room dormitory for Harvey Girls and other female employees of the Fred Harvey Company. Named for its architect, Mary Colter, it is a two- and three-story building with two wings, built of random cut-stone masonry, board-and-batten siding, and elaborately decorated railings.

EL TOVAR HOTEL

Architect Charles Whittlesey designed the four-story El Tovar Hotel (at right, circa 1920) as a compromise between ornate Swiss chalets and the more temperate rustic structures that by the 1920s would come to represent the NPS Rustic style. Below: Visitors on the east veranda of the hotel in 1906.

FOR A FEW YEARS following the arrival of Grand Canyon Railway in 1901, tourist activities were focused along the rim in the vicinity of Bright Angel Lodge, Kolb Studio, and Bright Angel Trail. Railroad officials redirected the action a quarter mile east when they opened El Tovar Hotel and Hopi House in January 1905.

For several decades thereafter, most visitors who came by rail stayed in the $250,000, one-hundred-room El Tovar, dawdling in its elegant restaurant, art galleries, roof-top gardens, solarium, and music, wine, billiard, and "rendezvous" rooms. Conversation and quiet contemplation on the east and north verandas were also popular pastimes. Most people arranged for guided trips along scenic drives to Hermits Rest, Desert View, and the Painted Desert, or booked a nine-hour mule ride to the Colorado River via the Bright Angel Trail. The circular drive fronting the hotel bustled with mule trains, horse-drawn buggies, and Fred Harvey touring cars, as well as guests.

Today the ambience surrounding the historic hotel has changed very little. People still creep or leap with mixed emotions toward the edge for their first glimpse of the abyss. In 1909 author John McCutcheon stood "gaping at the frightful immensity of the view" yet worshipped the inner-canyon's "gigantic mountain peaks painted all the colors of the rainbow." Others since have succumbed to vertigo, dropped to their knees and cried, fallen immediately in love, or quickly grown weary of a "hole a mile deep and thirteen miles wide." One visiting engineer offered to fill the cavity for a dollar per cubic yard.

PHOTO BY MIKE BUCHHEIT

Above: El Tovar today. Below: By 1910 El Tovar had become a part of the cultural landscape at Grand Canyon.

When El Tovar opened in 1905, it offered an unprecedented level of comfort to Grand Canyon visitors. Rooms were furnished with sleigh beds, the spacious dining room offered views of the canyon (as it does today), and the kitchen (bottom left) allowed for meals that met Fred Harvey's high standards. In 1906 the Santa Fe Railroad commissioned artist Louis Akin to produce a painting of the newly completed El Tovar (above). John G. Verkamp, one of three brothers who moved to Flagstaff, Arizona, from Cincinnati, Ohio, in the late 1800s, offered native hand crafts and other souvenirs to visitors. He briefly ran his store from a tent, circa 1898 (at right), then returned to build the current Verkamps Curios. The eclectic building has been described as a "modified-mission" design. It is unique at the South Rim for its roof, crafted to direct rainfall to a cistern beneath the porch. John and wife Catherine's descendants still own the store—the sole surviving family-owned concession at Grand Canyon National Park.

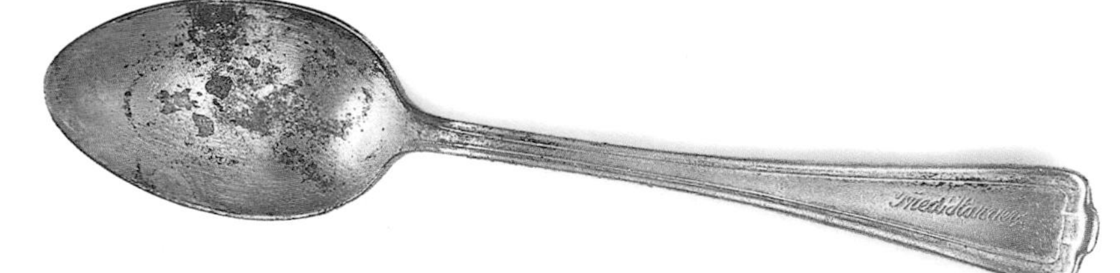

Architect Mary Colter, in her first major assignment at Grand Canyon, crafted Hopi House in a manner reminiscent of ancient southwestern pueblos. The style may appear incongruous with the adjacent El Tovar, but a century ago Whittlesey's accommodations catered to upscale tastes while Colter's effort jibed with easterners' emerging interest in southwestern Indian arts and crafts, avidly promoted by the railroad and Fred Harvey Company. The Hopi House offered, as it does today, a marvelous selection of crafts, but it also was home to working Hopi artisans (on the roof of Hopi House in 1905, at right) and performers who informed as well as entertained. For many years Navajo rug weavers and silversmiths lived and worked nearby in traditional hogans.

6

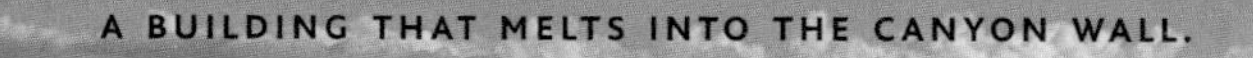

THE LOOKOUT, as it was originally known, is one of seven South Rim buildings designed by Santa Fe Railroad architect Mary Colter during 1905-37. Like many Colter creations, it mimics the architecture of twelfth-century southwestern peoples, with imperfect stone walls, flat roof, peeled-log timbers, and simple interior decoration. It is one of few rimside buildings that meld with the surrounding landscape, conforming to nineteenth-century landscape architect Frederick Law Olmsted's vision of unobtrusive amenities in the national parks.

Completed in 1914, Lookout Studio is reminiscent of the less-crowded, less-hurried South Rim experience of the 1900s to the 1930s. Imagine men and women dressed in eastern finery ambling west from El Tovar Hotel along a rim walk of wood planks, pausing here for an hour or an entire afternoon. An early Santa Fe Railroad promotional brochure suggested that visitors peer through telescopes to vicariously "traverse the Canyon trails, explore the rugged portions of the interior, or see its faraway reaches." A higher percentage of visitors then than now rode mules down to Indian Garden, Plateau Point, and Phantom Ranch, and The Lookout offered a pre-trip glimpse or post-trip mental reenactment of their adventure.

Others with curtailed itineraries curled up beside The Lookout's expansive windows to read from its library of canyon-related topics, or wrote letters and verse while pondering the precipice at their elbows. In the late evening it was customary to turn telescopes skyward for a bit of stargazing, all the while warmed by an open fireplace that cast its inviting glow throughout interior rooms.

The Lookout offered paintings, postcards, and photographs, competing with pioneer concessions run by the Kolb and Verkamp families, but competition was not its primary purpose. The building illustrates the railroad's ambition, adopted by the early National Park Service, to slow the pace of hurried travelers at rustic structures and scenic points, guiding them toward the long contemplation that Grand Canyon demands in order to be appreciated.

Above: In the telescope tower at Lookout Studio, 1915.
Below: Lookout Studio interior, 1915.

7 KOLB STUDIO

ELLSWORTH AND EMERY KOLB REACHED THE RIM IN 1901-02. THEIR STUDIO STILL STANDS, TODAY HOME TO A GALLERY AND BOOKSTORE.

VILLAGE DEVELOPMENT began in the winter of 1890-91 when prospectors Pete Berry and Ralph and Niles Cameron improved a centuries-old Havasupai route from Indian Garden to the rim. They named their new path the Bright Angel Toll Road. Often called "Cameron's Trail" before acquiring its current name, the Bright Angel Trail was traveled in the 1890s by prospectors, regional residents who wintered livestock on the Tonto Platform, and a few early tourists. With the promise of a railroad from Williams in the late 1890s, the Camerons improved the inner-canyon passage and extended it to the river, then erected a tent camp at Indian Garden and a hotel at the rim by 1903. The hand-hewn-log first floor of the

Emery photographed parties embarking down the trail on mules, then trotted four and a half miles (and more than three thousand vertical feet) to the nearest fresh water at Indian Garden to develop the film. Top: Edith Kolb, daughter of Emery and Blanche Kolb, as a child at Indian Garden, 1908. Above: Blanche Kolb at Indian Garden, 1910. Right: Kolb Studio in 1904, at the head of the Bright Angel Toll Road. Bottom: Emery Kolb in 1916, with the canvas boat he hand-carried down the Bright Angel Trail to cross the Colorado River.

The historic landscape surrounding Kolb Studio has changed considerably over the past century, but splendid views from the canyon's edge endure. The Rim Trail to the west climbs nearby Hopi Hill, affording panoramas of the inner-canyon corridor to Bright Angel Point on the North Rim. Visible from the studio itself are switchbacks of the Bright Angel Trail to Indian Garden, the Battleship (named after the Battleship *Iowa*) beneath Maricopa Point directly north, and Cheops Pyramid, as well as the buttes flanking Bright Angel Canyon north of the Colorado River. Above: Ellsworth and Emery Kolb, 1913.

former two-story hotel, used as the village post office during 1910-35, today serves as a Bright Angel Lodge guest cabin.

Ellsworth Kolb arrived in late 1901 amidst the flurry of tourist preparations and was joined by his brother Emery the following year. Like others who reached the rim in these years, the young men pondered ways to exploit the imminent tourism boom. They settled eventually on photography. Ralph Cameron gave them their start in late 1903 in a tent cabin beside his hotel, and in 1904 he allowed them to build a permanent studio on one of his mining claims at the chasm's very edge. In 1903 a bitter rivalry for tourist dollars erupted, with the Camerons and Kolbs teamed against the Santa Fe Railroad, Fred Harvey Company, and Martin Buggeln, proprietor of the Bright Angel Hotel. The struggle for village control derived from Cameron's imposition of a one-dollar trail toll, collected often as not by the Kolbs or Niles Cameron at a gate beside Kolb Studio. Ralph Cameron kept his toll, mining claims, and other holdings throughout early battles fought in Arizona's territorial courts, but he was finally ousted by the U.S. Supreme Court, U.S. Attorney General, and the National Park Service in the 1920s. Emery Kolb, wife Blanche, and daughter Edith, on the other hand, remained for decades to photograph and entertain tens of thousands of South Rim visitors. The studio was expanded in stages during 1904-26. It was acquired by the National Park Service after Emery's death in 1976 and was renovated by Grand Canyon Association in the 1990s. Today it houses a small bookstore and gallery.

MASWIK LODGE AND VICINITY

THE VILLAGE TODAY BLENDS PAST AND PRESENT.

DURING THE PRE-PARK ERA the grounds surrounding the Grand Canyon Railway wye were littered with trash heaps, septic settling ponds, railway debris, and construction camps where transient workers dabbled in bootleg whiskey and other nefarious enterprises. Today trains still pull into the wye beside Maswik Transportation Center and back up to the Santa Fe Railroad depot for the return run to Williams, but the landscape has improved remarkably.

In the 1930s the National Park Service and Fred Harvey Company developed the area northeast of the motor lodge for employee housing and a recreational area. The two-story village Community Building west of the mule barn and just north of Maswik Transportation Center, finished in 1935 with New Deal funds and craftsmen, served residents as a public meeting hall, auditorium, and movie theater into the late twentieth century. Allowed to deteriorate over the years, it was entirely renovated by Grand Canyon Association and Grand Canyon National Park Foundation in the 1990s.

The concrete block building west of the community center is Victor Hall, designed by Mary Colter in 1936 as the Fred Harvey men's dormitory. Conceptually it is similar to Colter's dormitory for women (Colter Hall), completed in the following year below El Tovar Hotel. The stucco-sheathed, two-story frame dormitory west of Victor Hall, built in 1913 beside El Tovar, was moved to this location in 1938, renovated, and renamed Victor Hall Annex.

A short walk north along Village Loop Drive leads across the tracks to Kolb Studio, Bright Angel trailhead, and the beginning of Hermit Road.

In 1926-27 the Santa Fe Railroad and the Fred Harvey Company reacted to the looming automobile age by building what they called the "motor lodge" or "auto camp," a precursor of today's motels. The original lodge (above, circa 1927), torn down to make way for Maswik Lodge, was once surrounded by as many as 150 single, duplex, and fourplex cabins, a few of which still stand in rows north of Maswik Lodge. The NPS public campground was moved here as well in 1927, occupying the area west of the cabins until Mather Campground was completed in the 1960s.

9 MULE BARNS AND VICINITY

Artist's conception of the proposed Fred Harvey livery area, including mule and horse barns, in 1905, two years prior to its completion.

WHEN SANTA FE RAILROAD officials began to develop the village, their general idea of traffic flow consisted of ushering guests from the train depot up the stairs to El Tovar Hotel. From there visitors could stroll along the canyon's edge and arrange for rides into the canyon and along scenic drives. No thought was given to tourists entering the industrial area south of the tracks, set aside for employee housing, railway structures, other service facilities, and seamier necessities like septic settling ponds and trash dumps.

National Park Service administrators removed most of these early structures, but a few of them survive beside Village Loop Drive between Center Road and Maswik Lodge. The horse and mule barns (built circa 1907) still stand on their original foundations north of this stretch of the drive, as does the blacksmith's shop (built circa 1908), just across the road and south of the barns. In the first decades of the twentieth century, wranglers saddled horses and hitched others to buggies to serve guests intent on scenic rides. Other wranglers who doubled as inner-canyon guides selected mule strings each morning then led them across the tracks to Bright Angel and El Tovar Hotels, where they would match the animals' size and temperament with their riders. In the years since then, guests, guides, and mules have met in the stone corral at the head of Bright Angel Trail for the same time-honored, often humorous ritual.

Other Fred Harvey service structures of the early park era lie just north of the barns. Three were designed in 1925, most likely by Santa Fe Railroad architect William H. Mohr. The massive powerhouse (1926) once held panels that controlled and conditioned the flow of potable water from Indian Garden, three thousand vertical feet below, to the rim. It also housed massive turbines that generated all of the village's electric power and steam heat. For many years the laundry plant (1926) immediately west of the powerhouse met the needs of a resort village with as many as five thousand daily visitors. The building south of the laundry (1931) was once the center of Fred Harvey maintenance activities. All three, like El Tovar Hotel, represent the railroad's predilection for Swiss chalet-style buildings of rustic stone and timber.

The first village development plan, prepared in 1924, envisioned an administrative or "first contact" zone surrounding the intersection of Center Road and Village Loop Drive. By 1928 contractors had finished the park's first automotive entrance road (today's Center Road) to replace pioneer paths of the horse-and-buggy era. From 1929 until 1954 all visitors arriving by commercial bus or private conveyance stopped at the administration building (today's Ranger Office) for information, and perhaps wandered across the street to Babbitt's Store (no longer standing) for groceries and other supplies. They then drove around the village loop to reach the garage and gas station, accommodations and restaurants along the rim, the public campground and early motor lodge at the site of today's Maswik Lodge, and scenic drives leading west to Hermits Rest and east to Desert View.

Automobiles climbing Hopi Hill on the old Hermit Rim Road in 1920.

Scenic tours west of Grand Canyon Village date to Sanford Rowe, a retired buffalo hunter who opened Rowe Well Camp three miles south of the rim in 1892. Rowe pioneered a path directly to Hopi Point—called Rowes Point back then—and led equestrian trips beside the abyss and down the Bright Angel Trail. Martin Buggeln, manager of the Bright Angel Hotel, cleared a crude wagon road from the village to Hopi Point around 1902. The Santa Fe Land Improvement Company (a subsidiary of the Santa Fe Railroad) surfaced Buggeln's road with volcanic cinders in 1907-08, then reconstructed and extended it to Hermits Rest in 1911-12.

The Santa Fe Railroad's Hermit Rim Road, twelve feet wide with eight-foot shoulders, was touted as a "city boulevard in the wilderness," and as safe as "an easy chair back home." Not quite—but it was a beautiful road for its time, the best in northern Arizona, designed by landscape architect George E. Kessler and the U.S. Forest Service to hug the rim yet spare the landscape. It was built in an era when most visitors arrived at the village by rail and signed up for half-day, leisurely horse-drawn buggy rides to

Hopi Hill ($1.50), Mohave Point ($2.00), and Hermits Rest ($3.00), often continuing down Hermit Trail to the Tonto Platform for a few days' stay at Hermit Camp.

The "city boulevard" immediately crumbled when it opened to automobiles in 1919. Although the National Park Service widened, oiled, then paved the road in the 1920s, it could not keep pace with increasing numbers of motorists who refused to heed the twelve-miles-per-hour speed limit. The road was entirely rebuilt to automotive standards in 1934-35 with depression-era highway funds ($185,000) and renamed West Rim Drive. The Bureau of Public Roads widened the roadway, reduced grades to 7 percent, and exercised extraordinary care not to mar adjacent vegetation. In the same years, park service crews improved a footpath immediately beside the rim as far as Hopi Point and later extended it all the way to Hermits Rest.

Today's seven-mile Hermit Road is essentially the same as the one completed in 1935. Shuttles, bicyclists, and pedestrians labor up the grade, crossing the Bright Angel Fault to gain the high ground atop Hopi Hill, pausing perhaps at Trailview I, Trailview II, Maricopa Point, and Powell Memorial along the way. Once on top, the road winds quite a bit on relatively flat ground for the remaining distance to Mohave Point, the Abyss, Pima Point, and Hermits Rest.

Elevations range from 6,600 feet at Hermits Rest to 7,100 feet at Hopi Point, not quite as high as Desert View Drive but nonetheless chilly in winter. For the entire route you are traveling through a life zone of pinyon pine and Utah juniper, drought-

Left: Carriages on the new road built by the Santa Fe Land Improvement Company in 1911 along the West Rim (today's Hermit Road). Above: Log arch over the entrance to the Hermit Rim Road, circa 1925-30.

resistant and enduring trees that often appear tortured by life beside the canyon edge but are well suited to the semi-arid land. You may see or hear flocks of jays harvesting nutrient-rich pinyon nuts or Townsend's solitaires plucking gin-flavored juniper berries in winter. It's more likely that you'll see white-throated swifts or violet-green swallows. See pages 70-71 for a pictorial inventory of some of the most common trees and frequently seen birds on the South Rim. Frequent western exposures beyond Hopi Point afford sunny moments on a slab of Kaibab Limestone, with views downriver into the deep backcountry of western Grand Canyon.

Visitors come to the canyon and Hermit Road for the breathtaking views and informal lessons in geology; both are found here in abundance. But don't ignore the relics of those who, long ago, opened the region to development and the rim to visitation. Most of the stone and masonry parapets along the rim and retaining walls at the overlooks were built in the 1930s by men of the Civilian Conservation Corps. Nine-foot pullouts beside the road reflect an era of fewer, slow-going, and narrow motor vehicles like Ford's Model A. There is a memorial to a courageous group of rag-tag river runners here, debris from one of the Southwest's richest uranium mines (best seen from the overlook at

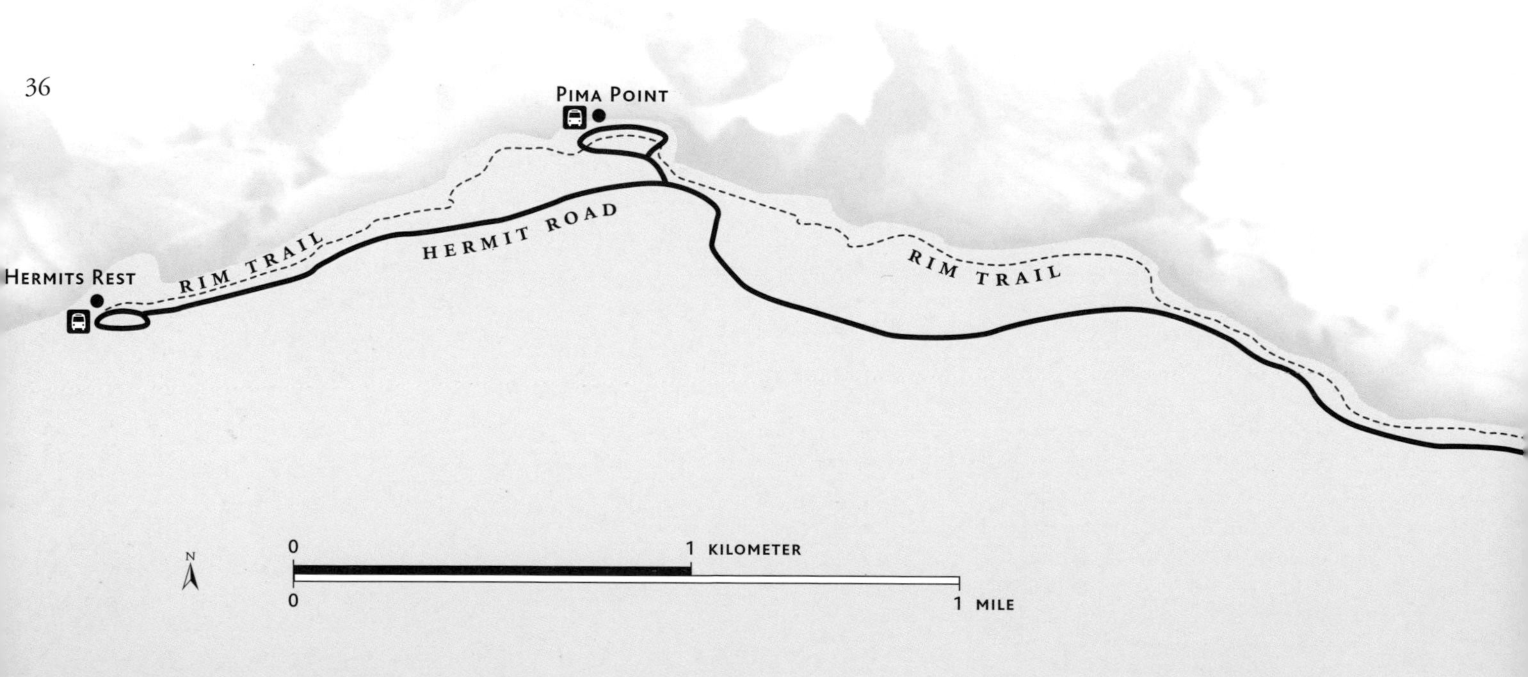

Maricopa Point), and a rest house built at trail's end, the work of one of the nation's first woman architects, and a fine one at that. Canyon scenery gave birth to its history, but the two are entwined.

NOTE: *Hermit Road is closed to private automobile traffic for most of the year. Check the park newspaper,* THE GUIDE, *for details and shuttle schedules.*

A SAFETY CAUTION

Hermit Road and the footpath alongside it seem perilously close to the edge at times, and looks do not deceive.

Not long ago, a young bicyclist let his attention drift and woke up (thankfully) on a talus slope staring up at the rim. Be careful. Pullouts and scenic stops have guardrails and viewing platforms, but use extra caution elsewhere.

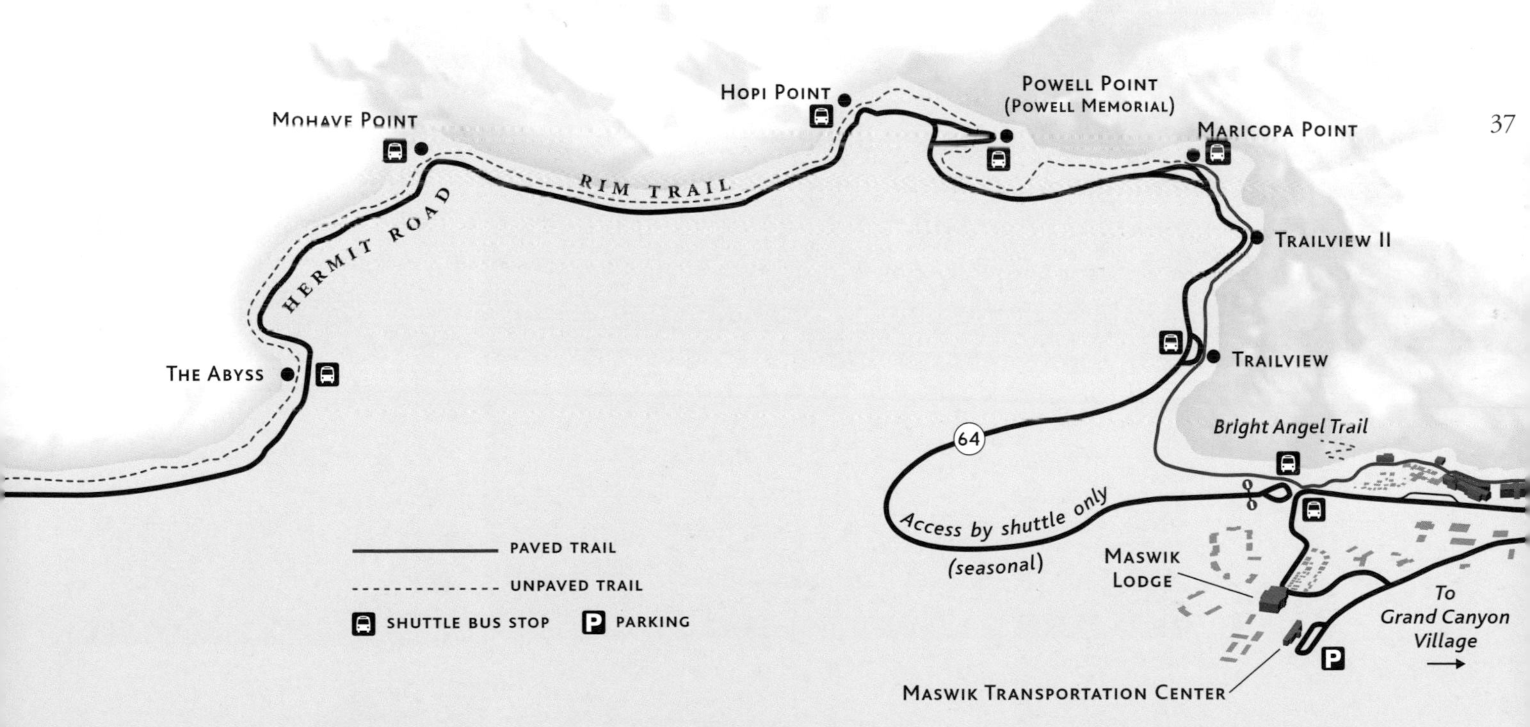

TRAILVIEW OVERLOOKS

SOME OF THE BEST SCENIC AND HISTORIC VIEWS ON THE SOUTH RIM.

Trailview overlooks provide the best views of the precipitous Bright Angel Trail. Mules descend the Bright Angel Trail each morning; those returning from Phantom Ranch ascend via the South Kaibab Trail. Most hikers make this same trip in reverse. Right: NPS ranger Pat Fenton with a visitor on the Bright Angel Trail, circa 1905.

THE TRAILVIEW OVERLOOKS and the Rim Trail in between divulge some of the best scenic and historic landscapes on the South Rim. On the horizon to the southeast are the San Francisco Peaks, a range of volcanic mountains sixty-five miles away. Red Butte, in the foreground, is an erosional sandstone remnant that owes its existence to a lava cap, all that remains

of flows from the San Francisco Peaks that once extended that far north. Closer still lies historic Grand Canyon Village, from Verkamps Curios on the east to Kolb Studio dangling over the edge to the west.

Bright Angel Trail plummets from the village to Indian Garden, the verdant patch below, before disappearing into Tapeats Narrows along Garden Creek. The 7.8-mile trail ends at the Colorado River, but transcanyon hikers continue along the River Trail and the North Kaibab Trail to reach the North Rim. This twenty-three-mile trail corridor follows the trace of the Bright Angel Fault, a fracture in the earth's crust that extends on both sides of the canyon. Such faults exist throughout the canyon, and where they occur, they facilitate the erosion of side canyons. First wildlife, then early American Indians wore paths to the river through these side canyons. Later, European American entrepreneurs rebuilt some of these paths to facilitate their money-making ventures.

When prospectors Pete Berry and Ralph Cameron improved the Havasupai route from Indian Garden to the rim in 1890-91, they did not realize that they had influenced the course of South Rim development. Cameron extended the trail to the river in 1898-99, filing mining claims along its length, then imposed a one dollar toll in 1903. As one early visitor described it, tourists for the next three decades "marched bravely out of the hotel, garbed in borrowed or extemporized riding outfit," rode mules down Cameron's two-foot-wide "snow-covered icy trail that zig zags down at a dizzy angle," and were grateful to get out alive. Then as now, the Fred Harvey cowboy guide cheerfully gave "the required information, whether he knows it or not."

The National Park Service finally gained control of the trail in 1928, then rebuilt it to ease the grades and overall experience. Gazing down you can still spot mule parties along with backpackers and day hikers who supply the comparative scale required to appreciate just how grand the canyon is.

Above left: At the head of the Bright Angel Trail, circa 1915. Above right: A group of trail riders approaches the head of the Bright Angel Trail in 1952. Left: A group from the Los Angeles Chamber of Commerce visits the inner canyon in 1906. In the absence of a bridge or tramway, visitors to the bottom of the canyon spent a bit of time on the banks of the Colorado River, then headed back up the Bright Angel Trail.

A PIECE OF MINING HISTORY

THE LANDSCAPE immediately west of Maricopa Point was at one time the scene of the most intensive mining activity ever to take place at Grand Canyon National Park. The story begins with Daniel Lorain Hogan, a Flagstaff deputy sheriff and part-time prospector who discovered green mineral stains (a signature for copper ore) 1,100 feet below this overlook in 1890. Three years later, Hogan filed the twenty-acre Orphan mining claim that extended from his initial prospect up to and including four acres atop the rim. He converted the parcel to private property in 1906. President Theodore Roosevelt, who had served as his commanding officer in the Spanish-American War, personally signed the papers.

Hogan rarely shipped copper but clung to his tract while other South Rim pioneers died, were displaced, or moved away of their own accord. In 1936 he opened a tourist facility at the rim that grew under successive managers (one of whom was Will Rogers, Jr.) to consist of twenty cabins, a trading post, and saloon. Hogan finally sold out in 1947 (for about $25,000) to Mrs. Madelaine Jacobs. She discovered that the gray rock kicked aside for decades contained some of the richest uranium ore in the Southwest. Jacobs sold to Western Gold and Uranium, Inc., and from 1956 until 1969 half a million tons of Grand Canyon ore helped fuel the nation's atomic energy program.

Above: Dan Hogan's Hummingbird Trail, 1913. Right: Artist's conception of the luxury hotel, proposed in the 1960s, that would cascade down the canyon's edge below Maricopa Point "like a waterfall."

Above: The headframe at the Orphan Mine as it appeared in 1978. Below: Underground schematic of the Orphan Mine.

Had you visited the South Rim in the 1950s and 1960s, you might have rubbed shoulders with the Orphan Mine's rowdy off-duty miners at the Bright Angel Lodge lounge. You would have seen, perhaps breathed, the radioactive dust and felt the ore laden trucks rumble through the village day and night on their way to the refinery at Tuba City. When, by the late 1960s, a reduced demand for uranium ended the mining venture, owners announced plans to build a luxury hotel that would have dwarfed El Tovar and cascaded over the canyon's edge "like a waterfall." That's when Congress passed a law to purchase the property, close the tourist camp, and terminate mineral rights. In 1987 the private inholding became a part of the national park. Several private parcels still exist within the park, but it's a pretty sure bet that something like the Orphan Mine will never reoccur.

Today a careful eye can detect the yawning vertical shaft well below Maricopa Point to the west, along with cables and the dilapidated superstructure of a tram that once serviced the mine. Close inspection of rimside debris is not possible; the site is fenced and closed to the public because of the (minimal) danger of radioactivity.

12 POWELL POINT AND MEMORIAL

A MONUMENT TO THE FIRST COLORADO RIVER RUNNER, JOHN WESLEY POWELL.

NUMEROUS MONUMENTS to canyon historical figures are found within the park. None approaches the size and prominence of Powell Memorial, erected in 1915 to honor the first party to run the Colorado River through Grand Canyon and their leader, John Wesley Powell. This is also the site of the park's formal dedication in 1920, attended by Powell's niece and grand-niece as well as a multitude of state and federal dignitaries.

Powell, a self-taught scientist and major of artillery in the Civil War, set out from Green River, Wyoming, in May 1869 with four wooden boats and nine steely men to explore the untested Colorado River as far as the Mormon settlements below Grand Canyon. Three months later, only six near-naked, half-starved survivors and two battered boats emerged from the canyon's portal at Grand Wash Cliffs, minus most of their equipment and scientific notations. Powell returned with an entirely new crew in 1871 and completed a more thorough, less eventful examination of the river environs and Grand Canyon's north rim. Powell went on to become the first director of the Bureau of Ethnology, second director of the U.S. Geological Survey, and a staunch advocate for the conservation of public lands, until his death in 1902.

Most everyone agreed that Powell and his men deserved a memorial to their accomplishments, but some disagreed at the time with the decision to ignore the four men who did not complete the first trip; their names do not appear on the monument. Frank Goodman,

Top: H.P. Mollhausen's engraving of the canyons below Grand Canyon from the Ives expedition in 1857. Ives's visit to the canyon predated Powell's by twelve years. Above: Powell's pocket watch, from the 1869 expedition. Right: Beaman photo of "our first camp" from the second Powell expedition, 1871.

who joined at Green River on the spur of the moment, left after the first major rapid and perhaps deserved the slight. But brothers Oramel and Seneca Howland and William Dunn were labeled "deserters" for exiting only a few days before the end of the trip, a decision they paid for with their lives.

Controversy surrounds the fate of Dunn and the Howlands after they escaped the canyon to the north onto the Shivwits Plateau. The traditional story, originating with Mormon scout Jacob Hamblin in 1870, is that they were murdered by Southern Paiutes who were not on good terms with white men at the time. More recently, some have surmised that the men may have been killed by Mormons who thought them spies for an unfriendly federal government. Lively controversies like these contribute to the fascinating lore of the Colorado River.

This site also reminds us of all the lesser-known river runners who followed in Powell's wake: the Kolb brothers and Than Galloway, Robert Stanton and George Flavell, Buzz Holmstrom, James Best, Julius Stone, and dozens more who ran the river when the river ran wild.

Left: Clement Powell's journal, from the second Powell expedition, 1871-72. Below: The Kolb brothers at the foot of the Bass Trail, 24 December 1911. By the time the Kolbs made their historic canyon journey, only a handful of people had ever traversed the Colorado River through Grand Canyon.

13

HOPI POINT

THE OVERLOOK AT HOPI POINT *extends farther into the canyon* **THAN ANY OTHER ALONG HERMIT ROAD.**

The view downriver, 1930. Photo by George Grant.

HOPI POINT was initially named Rowes Point for Sanford Rowe, an immigrant from the Great Plains who opened a tourist facility several miles south of the village in 1892. Rowe cleared an equestrian path north from his camp to this site and was the first to provide guided trips into the canyon over the Bright Angel Trail. Hopi Point was also the terminus of guided tours west of the village until the Santa Fe Railroad completed Hermit Rim Road in 1912. Hopi Point has been home to fire lookout towers since the turn of the century.

Pioneer guides and forest rangers who staffed the lookout towers gravitated here because the overlook extends farther into the canyon than others along Hermit Road and offers some of the best unobstructed views. As the Fred Harvey Company advertised nearly a century ago,

> *the panorama here, in broad daylight, seems to be the acme of scenic beauty. But when the afternoon sun . . . gradually sinks beneath the far mountain ranges, banked with clouds . . . the Canyon depths become a world of mystery, with giant forms dimly outlined in the ghostly void. And then, miracle of miracles! the western sky becomes a riot of vivid colors, flaming across a field of turquoise, and fading to the afterglow.*

Such a deal for $1.50, round-trip from El Tovar! We seldom write like that anymore, but it is all true. Views to the west extend to Mt. Trumbull, sixty miles distant, and beyond to the Kanab and Shivwits Plateaus. The western panorama at sundown indeed supplies a "riot of vivid colors" if conditions are right, but the view facing east, away from the setting sun toward Cape Royal, Vishnu Temple, and Wotans Throne, is consistently spectacular. The rock appears to blush, shadows are accentuated, and perspective is distorted. Hermit and Granite Rapids are visible a vertical mile below, flanked by the forbidding dark schist of Granite Gorge. Hopi Point's long, lower tendril—Dana Butte—points across the river to Shiva Temple, soaring more than six hundred feet higher than Hopi Point.

Top: Ranger Pat Fenton with a group at Hopi Point in 1905. Below: The Alligator below Hopi Point.

A group from the Los Angeles Chamber of Commerce at Hopi Point in 1906.

14 MOHAVE POINT

An expansive view **OF THE CANYON DOWNRIVER.**

Top: Early tour buses at Mohave Point. Right: The view from Mohave Point in 1930. Photo by George Grant.

MANY OF GRAND CANYON'S major plateaus, buttes, "temples," spires, and rapids were named for or by early explorers or canyon residents who, overcome by the chasm's grandeur, waxed whimsical.

The Alligator, an imaginative title bestowed by long-time South Rim resident Emery Kolb, points north-northwest from below Mohave Point to an interesting group of inner-canyon monuments just across the Colorado River. These are the Tower of Set, named by landscape artist Thomas Moran, followed by Horus and Osiris Temples, named by Clarence Dutton following his early 1880s survey of the northwest canyon. Left of these three is the Tower of Ra, and, to the right, Isis Temple. One would have to be schooled in the classics, as Dutton was, to understand the tongue-in-cheek irony of placing these names together, as they represent a dysfunctional family of Egyptian deities: Isis was the daughter of Ra (the sun god) and wife of Osiris (god of the underworld). Osiris was murdered by his evil brother Set (god of war), and avenged by his son, Horus.

Other features visible from Mohave Point include the series of three rapids below and downstream: Salt Creek, Granite, and Hermit. Salt Creek was named by Dutton's geographer, Henry Gannet, for its taste. Granite Rapids, at the mouth of Monument Canyon immediately to the west, reflects the pink stone found in the walls of Granite Gorge. Hermit Rapid is named for canyon pioneer prospector and tourist guide Louis Boucher, who made his solitary home and living within the side canyons downstream in the years 1889-1912. An unassuming man, he nonetheless has the honor of the most canyon features named for him: three labeled Boucher (Creek, Trail, Rapids), nine titled Hermit (Road, Rest, Trail, Camp, Fault, Basin, Creek, Rapids, Shale), and Eremita (Spanish for Hermit) Mesa.

15

PIMA POINT

FROM PIMA POINT ON A STILL DAY YOU CAN HEAR THE SOFT ROAR OF GRANITE RAPID *5,000 feet below.*

Below: Superstructure of the tramway from Pima Point to Hermit Camp. At the time it was the longest single-span tram in the world. From 1926 to 1936 it supplied Hermit Camp and offered a terrifying twenty-minute joy ride for the few employees and village residents who dared. Right: Hermit Camp, 1913.

MANY SOUTH RIM VISITORS gaze longingly into the chasm and wonder why there are no aerial trams down to the Tonto Platform or Colorado River. There has never been a tram from rim to river, though one was begun in 1919 to span the entire canyon from Hopi Point to the North Rim. It surprises many to learn that there have been at least six cable systems that crossed the Colorado River at river level (two still exist at gauging stations), and four that descended from the rim to inner-canyon locations. Of the latter, all but one were temporary aids to mining operations or construction of water pipelines.

On March 26, 1926, infant Zona Carolyn Morris lay coddled in blankets at the very brink

of Pima Point when her father touched off a cannon launching a guide line into Hermit Basin to the west. The shot signaled the beginnings of a seven-eighths-inch steel-cable tramway that plummeted, without intermediate support towers, some six thousand feet to the Santa Fe Railroad's Hermit Camp. Hermit Camp itself was completed in 1912 as an upscale alternative to inner-canyon camps operated by canyon pioneers William Bass, Ralph Cameron, and David Rust. The Santa Fe Railroad invested $72,000 to build a dining hall, rows of tent cabins, a blacksmith's shop, restrooms and showers, and the tram itself. Guests usually spent a couple of days hiking Hermit Creek to the river or riding along the Tonto Trail that passed beside the camp. Many returned to the village by way of the Tonto and Bright Angel Trails. Hermit Camp was abandoned in 1930, and on a nippy November night in 1936, village residents huddled at Pima Point to watch the flames as Fred Harvey employees torched what they could not salvage. The tramway was severed and removed soon thereafter. The ruins of Hermit Camp are faintly visible below.

The Abyss is one of many deep "bays" that have been cut back into the South Rim by headward erosion from canyon tributaries—in this case, Monument Creek. Road builders of the 1930s generally placed narrow pullouts at these overlooks to invite intimate views, in contrast to the grander panoramas available at the "points." Here, the main attraction is the Great Mohave Wall, an almost sheer cliff plunging three thousand feet to the soft Bright Angel Shale that covers the Tonto Platform.

HERMITS REST

Hermits Rest in 1920.

IN 1909 the Santa Fe Railroad, with the encouragement of the U.S. Department of the Interior, undertook a major construction project that included a road west from Grand Canyon Village, a rest house at road's end, an 8.5-mile trail from its terminus down to the Tonto Platform, and an overnight camp at trail's end, all for the sole purpose of bypassing Ralph Cameron's Bright Angel Trail. They named these structures for Louis Boucher, nicknamed "the Hermit," an immigrant from Canada, part-time prospector, and full-time tourist guide who operated crude overnight camps below Hermits Rest at Dripping Springs and within Boucher Canyon.

The Santa Fe Railroad chose Mary Colter, Grand Canyon's most prolific architect, to design Hermits Rest as a "primitive" shelter built into the hillside, such that "from the road all that can be seen is a wooded knoll, with a cairn of rock for a chimney." It was a wearisome (if wonderful) trip along the dusty road in horse-drawn conveyances to Hermits Rest. Passengers could enjoy a respite here beneath the roofed-in porch in summer or beside the pinyon-fed fire in the massive interior fireplace in cooler weather. Snacks from the kitchenette fortified guests before their return to the village or for the journey down Hermit Trail by mule.

The path to Hermit Camp was hailed by all as a state-of-the-art backcountry trail, four feet wide with easy grades, paved with cobblestones,

and secured by stone walls on the outside. Along the way riders passed such colorful features as Trail Top Gulch, the White Zigzags, Big Jim Spring, Cathedral Stairs, Santa Maria Spring (with rest house), the Red Zigzags, and Breezy Point. Hermit Trail far surpassed the quality of earlier inner-canyon paths and served as a model for National Park Service trails built in the 1920s and 1930s.

Fred Harvey brochures proclaimed that Hermit Camp at the end of the trail represented "camping out de luxe," with a central dining hall and Fred Harvey chef, eleven tent cabins that accommodated thirty persons, stables, phones, showers, and restrooms. Tent cabins were furnished with "restful beds, rugs, and other conveniences."

Hermit Camp was abandoned in 1930, following construction of Phantom Ranch in 1922, completion of the South Kaibab Trail in 1925, and federal acquisition of the Bright Angel Trail in 1928. It was intentionally burned to the ground in 1936.

Top left: The fireplace at Hermits Rest, circa 1915. Left: Hermits Rest in 1936. Photo by George Grant. Below left: Boucher's camp at Dripping Springs west of the Hermit Trail. Below: The interior of Hermits Rest, circa 1916.

A Civilian Conservation Corps crew constructing guardrails along the East Rim Drive (today's Desert View Drive), 1938.

James Thurber, proprietor of the Tolfree tourist camp near Grandview Point in the late 1890s, extended the Flagstaff-Grandview stage road to the Bright Angel trailhead in 1896. After the arrival of Grand Canyon Railway in 1901 and subsequent development of Grand Canyon Village, tourism operators like Pete Berry and the Fred Harvey Company improved the path and extended it east to scenic overlooks at Lipan Point and Desert View. Automobiles braved the route after 1910, but it remained little more than an eight-foot-wide, sinuous set of wagon tracks through ponderosa pine forest spotted with steep limestone gullies, impassable in winter and difficult the remainder of the year.

By 1919 the "El Tovar-Desert View Road" was still nothing to boast about. Coconino County and the U.S. Forest Service refused to

spend a dime on maintenance, relying on Fred Harvey crews to keep it passable for scenic tours. Harvey tours included pack trips that more often followed a nearby American Indian trade trail to the Desert View vicinity and continued to the Hopi villages for $5 per day plus provisions. Two- or three-day wagon trips to Desert View cost the same. One-day motor tours, on the other hand, cost $10 per person (about two days' wages). Because of frequent breakdowns and other difficulties, drivers carried passenger pigeons to signal for help, and passengers rented linen dusters, hats, and goggles as protection from the mud and dust.

Little changed in the few years following arrival of the National Park Service. Rangers took over road maintenance within the park while Fred Harvey spent more than $40,000 building and maintaining a somewhat better Navahopi Road to the Painted Desert during 1924-29. Motor trips remained adventures, however, with speed limits ranging from eight miles per hour when approaching horse-drawn conveyances (which had the right-of-way), to twelve miles per hour on steep grades and sharp turns, to twenty miles per hour when no other vehicle was within two hundred yards. Motorists sounded their horns at thirty degree blind curves and cooled their brakes at the bottom of 8 percent grades before moving on.

Today's Desert View Drive dates to the years 1927-31, when the National Park Service and federal Bureau of Public Roads completed four major automotive roads on the North and South Rims. The new highway to Desert View, called East Rim Drive until the end of the twentieth century, was designed by NPS engineers and landscape architects to follow a relatively straight and level alignment away from the canyon's edge for greater speed (thirty-five miles per hour) and to avoid scarring the landscape with excessive cuts and fills. But they placed the road close enough to the rim to allow for pullouts at scenic bays and short spur roads to scenic points. The road was widened and realigned in 1955-63 to indulge a faster (forty-five miles per hour) generation of motor vehicles and more hurried visitors, but the concept of alternating pullouts for intimate canyon views and scenic overlooks for grander vistas remains.

The original East Rim Drive began at the Fred Harvey Garage at Village Loop Drive and continued twenty-five miles east to its terminus at Desert View. Until the 1950s there were no developments immediately east of the village except the pioneer cemetery beside today's Shrine of the Ages. The first turnoff veered north to the park's first formal museum at Yavapai Point. Mather Point was not developed until 1953, so once past Yavapai, concession tours, "automotive caravans" led by NPS interpreters (until World War II), and private motorists continued east along the picturesque gravel road lined with rustic guard rails to

pause at essentially the same scenic points available today. The National Park Service and the Bureau of Public Roads completed a thirty-three-mile "mountain" highway from Desert View (7,438 feet) to Cameron (4,370 feet) in 1935, bypassing the hair-raising Navahopi Road and supplying motorists with an alternate, comfortable, and scenic passage to and from the South Rim.

Desert View Drive and its spurs to scenic points are open year-round but are subject to temporary closures in winter due to heavy snows. Elevations vary from 7,000 feet near the village to 7,500 feet at Navajo Point. Winter days can be very cold at dawn but are usually mild by mid-afternoon and tolerable until the early evening. Winter is a good time of year for photography; slanting rays cast long shadows all day long, and inner-canyon formations "seem to rise slowly from the depths, or step forward from hiding places" beside the North Rim. Summer mornings and evenings are temperate, though midday, as a Fred Harvey brochure put it, "is the time of least charm, for the depths have lost their defining shadows." Each named stop along Desert View Drive offers informative interpretive exhibits and the opportunity for panoramic views of the eastern Grand Canyon.

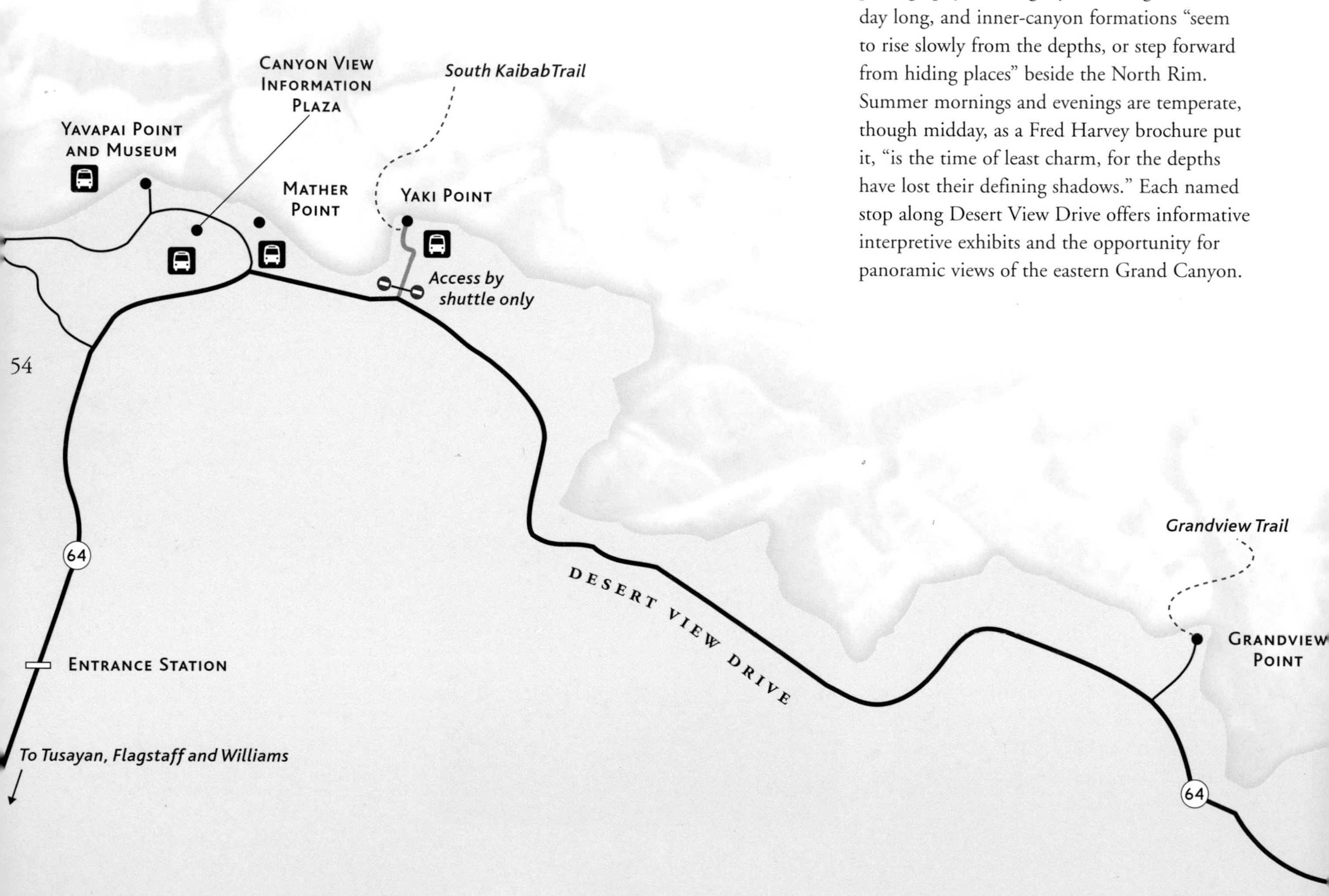

MARY COLTER, GRAND CANYON ARCHITECT

Grand Canyon's historic landscape is rich with the works of several prominent turn-of-the-century architects, none more original, prolific, and thought-provoking than Mary Elizabeth Jane Colter. Colter was born in Pittsburg, Pennsylvania, on 4 April 1869. Eschewing feminine roles of the late Victorian Era, she attended the California School of Design in the 1880s and worked as an apprentice designer in the 1890s, years when few men and fewer women were licensed as architects. Her first professional break came in 1902 when the Fred Harvey Company commissioned her to decorate the "Indian Building" next to the Alvarado Hotel in Albuquerque, New Mexico. Two years later Harvey hired Colter to decorate the interior of El Tovar Hotel, inaugurating her thirty-five-year relationship with Grand Canyon. Contemporaries described Colter as a feisty individual who used diplomacy to get what she wanted from management but often harangued artisans to ensure that her personal vision emerged from their labor. That vision focused on re-creations (not copies) of prehistoric and historic southwestern buildings using native materials and building techniques, sometimes incorporating structural errors to achieve authenticity.

The fact that all of Colter's Grand Canyon buildings still stand and serve historic functions, despite the changing cultural landscape of the past century, is testament to the high esteem others have held for her work. The developed South Rim is, in fact, framed by two of her designs—Hermits Rest (1914) on the west and the Watchtower (1932) on the east. In between at Grand Canyon Village you may discover and admire The Lookout (1914), Bright Angel Lodge (1935), El Tovar interior (1905), Hopi House (1905), Victor Hall (1936), and Colter Hall (1937). Mary Colter died at Santa Fe, New Mexico, on 8 January 1958.

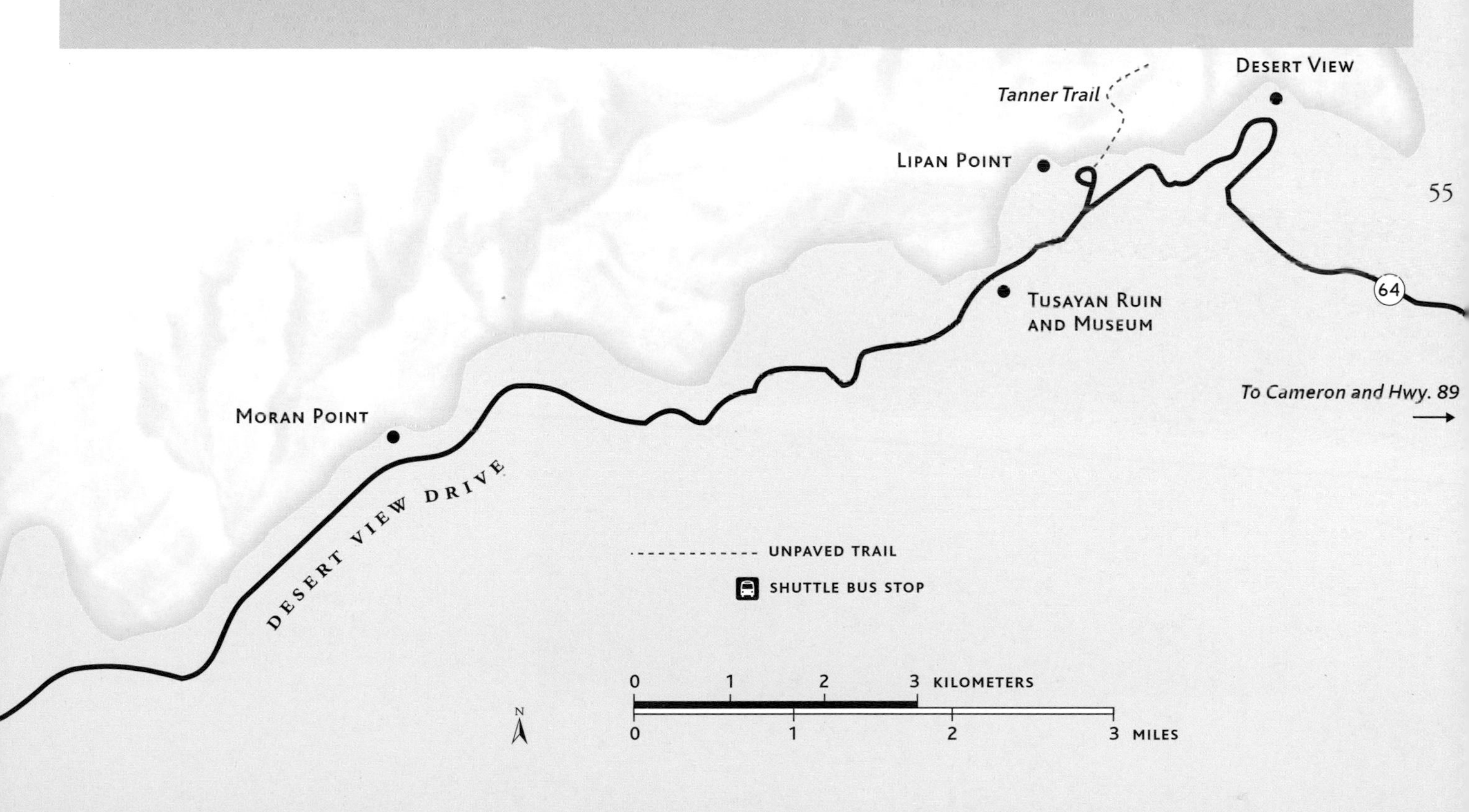

17

YAKI POINT

Right: Dr. David White and Dr. John C. Merriam, collecting fossil ferns from the Hermit Shale, at Cedar Ridge on the South Kaibab Trail, 1927. Left: Crinoid fossils from the Kaibab Limestone. Below: The South Kaibab Trail just above Cedar Ridge.

YAKI POINT *seems to hang in mid-air,* **OFFERING A FINE VIEW OF SPIRES, BUTTES, MESAS, AND TALUS SLOPES.**

THE SOUTH KAIBAB TRAIL, which descends into the canyon from Yaki Point, is an artifact of the early struggle between private and public interests to control South Rim tourism and inner-canyon access. The Santa Fe Railroad tried and failed to break pioneer entrepreneur Ralph Cameron's stranglehold on the Bright Angel toll trail by building its own Hermit Trail west of Grand Canyon Village in 1912. When Coconino County residents voted down a referendum to transfer the Bright Angel Trail to the federal government in 1924, the National Park Service immediately went to work building yet another bypass trail, this time from Yaki Point.

Most park trails follow the routes of earlier American Indian footpaths, but the seven-mile-long South Kaibab Trail, finished in June 1925 at a cost of $73,000, was blasted out of solid rock. The result is a trail that follows a ridgeline for much of its length, offering unparalleled views of the inner canyon. Workers (mostly Mormon residents of the Arizona Strip north of Grand Canyon) used technical innovations like portable compressors and jackhammers to chisel their way up from the river and down from Yaki Point, producing a four-and-a-half-foot-wide boulevard with grades of less than 17 percent. NPS and concessioner residences, barns, and corrals near the trailhead were finished between 1925-29.

Publicity battles continued between Coconino County and park administrators. Coconino County had acquired the Bright Angel Trail in 1906 (though Cameron continued to pocket the tolls for many years). Park administrators wanted the new "Yaki Trail" to eclipse the Bright Angel. The issue of control was finally resolved in 1928 when the county donated the Bright Angel Trail to the federal government in exchange for a park approach road from Williams. The park service went on to finish the North Kaibab Trail and Kaibab Suspension Bridge in 1928. They reconstructed the Bright Angel Trail during 1929-38 and supervised construction of the River Trail by the Civilian Conservation Corps in 1933-36, completing today's trans-canyon trail system.

Yaki Point juts so far into the canyon that it seems to hang in mid-air. The view provides fine perspectives of inner-canyon spires, buttes, and mesas, and an unobstructed glimpse of the South Rim's cliffs and talus slopes. The panorama stretches from Great Thumb Mesa in the west to the Palisades of the Desert east of Desert View. Clear Creek Canyon and the trail leading to it from Phantom Ranch are visible across the river along the Tonto Platform. Civilian Conservation Corps recruits who built the trail in the mid-1930s discovered four-thousand-year-old split-twig figurines in a cave beside the creek, providing the first evidence of Archaic peoples within Grand Canyon.

NOTE: *Check the park newspaper, THE GUIDE, for shuttle schedules to Yaki Point.*

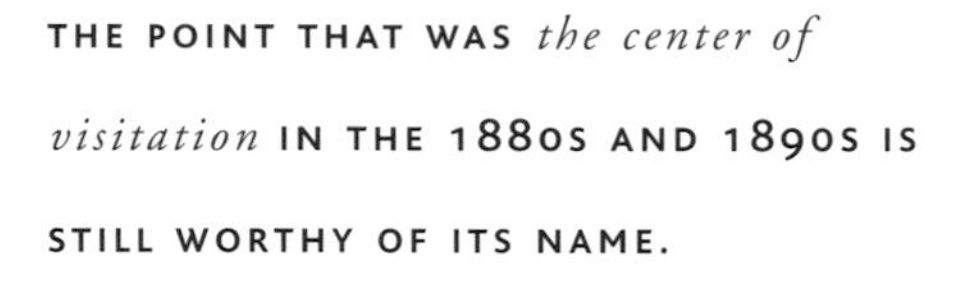

THE POINT THAT WAS *the center of visitation* **IN THE 1880S AND 1890S IS STILL WORTHY OF ITS NAME.**

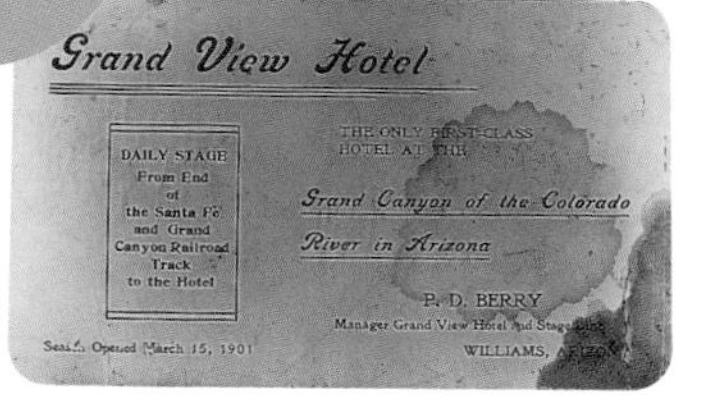

Below: Front of the Grand View Hotel, circa 1900. Right: The Canyon Copper Company dining room on Horseshoe Mesa, circa 1906. Nothing remains today of the dining room below the rim.

GRANDVIEW POINT was the locus of South Rim visitation from the mid-1880s through the early 1900s. Brothers Philip and William Hull ran a sheep ranch and part-time tourism venture with John Hance there, several miles back from the rim. Hance, the first white settler on the South Rim, arrived in 1883 and achieved notoriety regaling guests with tall tales at his rimside homestead and guiding visitors into the chasm along the Old and New Hance Trails. Williams businessman Martin Buggeln bought Hance's ranch in 1906 and ran cattle in the vicinity until his death thirty-three years later.

Others braved the wagon road from Flagstaff to seek their fortune here, but the most prominent was Peter D. Berry, who arrived with brothers Ralph and Niles Cameron in 1888 and remained until his death in 1932. Berry and his partners discovered a sizable copper vein below Grandview

Point in 1892 and finished the Grand View Toll Trail from Grandview Point to their claims on Horseshoe Mesa the following year.

In many ways, Berry was the archetypal South Rim pioneer. He ran a stable business (a saloon) in Flagstaff, but spent much of his time wandering the canyon's depths with pick, shovel, and pack burro, searching for the mother lode. When he thought he had found it, Pete worked from dawn to well after sunset trying to make it pay. Workers earned $4.00 per day to chisel copper ore, but hauling it up a 2,600-vertical-foot trail on the backs of mules, carting it sixty miles to the railroad, then paying freight to El Paso for refining proved a hard way to eke out a living.

Berry, like his fellow pioneers, had slightly better success as a canyon hostler and guide. He began leading visitors into the canyon as a sideline, then finished his rustic Grand View Hotel at the rim by 1897. The future looked cheery until the railway arrived thirteen miles west at what would become the new center of South Rim visitation. The business Pete and his wife Martha labored so hard to develop bled red ink for another decade then sputtered and died.

Little other than place names remains of the development at Grandview Point, but it is still a splendid experience to hike a ways down Pete Berry's Grandview Trail, following in the century-old steps of early tourists, miners, and pack mules. The trail's destination can be seen from the overlook—any idea how it got its name?

Interior of the Grand View Hotel, circa 1906.

MORAN POINT

A POINT NAMED TO HONOR ONE OF *many artists* WHO HAVE CAPTURED THE GLORIES OF THE CANYON IN PAINT.

Above: Thomas Moran and his daughters at the canyon, circa 1910. From 1899 to 1920 Moran spent nearly every winter at Grand Canyon. Bottom right: Gunnar Widforss, who lived and worked at Grand Canyon for many years, produced a body of work prized for its artistic elegance and geologic detail.

GRAND CANYON'S SOUTH RIM has been the inspiration for untold numbers of landscape artists who have tried to capture, embellish, or translate the stupendous scene on film or canvas. Heinrich Balduin Mollhausen and Baron Friedrich W. von Egloffstein, European artists who accompanied Lt. Joseph Ives's exploration of the lower Colorado River in 1857-58, were the first to try. Frederick Samuel Dellenbaugh, at seventeen years of age, joined the second Powell expedition through Grand Canyon and painted his impression of the Inner Gorge in 1875. His companion, Jack Hillers, took the first photographs, and fine ones they are. Other Grand Canyon artists include William Henry Holmes, who illustrated Clarence

Dutton's *Tertiary History of the Grand Cañon District* (1882), and Gunnar Mauritz Widforss, a canyon resident in the 1920s and 1930s, considered one of the most technically competent of canyon painters.

Experts write that the artist's challenge at Grand Canyon is to combine skill and personal insight with the variety and quality of light in boundless space. Our skill may be limited, but we can frame segments of the chasm in our minds or viewfinders, trying not to picture the grand panorama all at once. Focus on the brilliant glow of Red Canyon or Hance Rapid straight down from Moran Point, perhaps, or the Walhalla Plateau as it extends out to Wotans Throne and Vishnu Temple along the North Rim horizon. Soft morning, evening, and winter light cast complex shadows lending shape and depth to every cliff face, pinnacle, and cranny. The same light dances on multicolored strata and the velvety green river near Unkar Delta to the northeast. No quick glimpse and snapshot here; allow time for personal insight.

Above: A sketch of the Nankoweap Basin executed in 1882 by B.L. Young for C.D. Walcott. Right: *Zoroaster Temple*, by Gunnar Widforss.

TUSAYAN RUIN

A PLACE TO MEET SOME OF THE CANYON'S *earliest* INHABITANTS.

Tusayan Museum in 1932, the year it was completed.

EUROPEAN AMERICAN visitation and settlement is only the tip of the iceberg when it comes to the human history of Grand Canyon. Paleo-Indian hunters passed by not long after the end of the last ice age. The Archaic peoples who replaced them pursued a hunter-gatherer lifestyle for millennia thereafter. Nearly all of the more than three thousand prehistoric sites uncovered so far within the park, however, are associated with Puebloan cultures dating back two thousand years. Their population peaked around A.D. 1050-1150 then declined soon after the turn of the thirteenth century.

Elders who inhabited the village at Tusayan during 1185-1210 must have had some fascinating ancestral stories to tell their children, as they were among the last to hang on at Grand Canyon: twelve centuries of moving between the great chasm's rim and interior to hunt and snare small game and farm beside its springs, creeks, and river; the introduction of corns, beans, squash, and cotton over time and invention of check dams and terraces to allow farming within washes beside the rim; the development of bows and throwing sticks to improve the odds at hunting; a knowledge of hundreds of native plants, creation of complex religious beliefs, and expertise in utilitarian as well as elegant ceramic pottery. They responded to increased competition for marginal resources in a land that seemed to become drier by the century by starting over somewhere else using ever more sophisticated building techniques. They watched their society wither, then died or migrated east to live among the Hopis, Zunis, Acomas, and the inhabitants of the Pueblo villages along the Rio Grande River.

Tusayan Ruin was excavated in 1930 by a small team from Gila Pueblo in Globe, Arizona, led by Harold S. Gladwin and noted archaeologist Emil W. Haury. The adjacent interpretive center, built in 1932, was named the MacCurdy Wayside Museum of Archeology in honor of the woman who donated the $4,500 required for its construction. Interior displays and furnishings were originally crafted by artisans of the Civil Works Administration during the Great Depression. Today's museum exhibits and a self-guided tour through the remains of Tusayan Pueblo offer a comprehensive look at Grand Canyon's earliest residents.

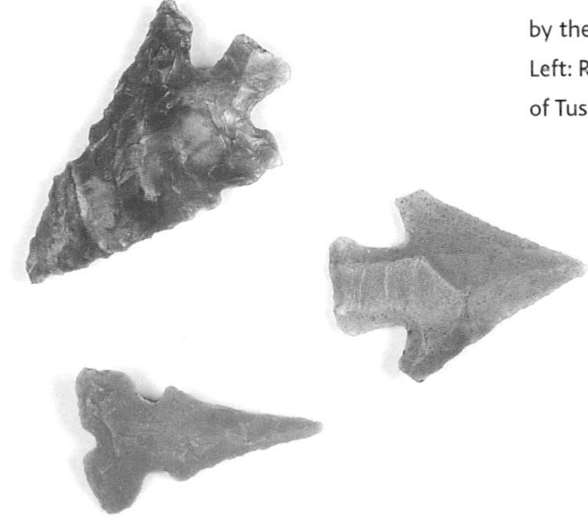

Above: Excavation of the Tusayan site by the staff from Gila Pueblo, 1930.
Left: Ranger Ed McKee at the remains of Tusayan Pueblo, 1931.

LIPAN POINT

THE MOST SPACIOUS VIEW FROM THE SOUTH RIM IS REVEALED BEYOND CÁRDENAS BUTTE.

DESERT VIEW DRIVE curls and climbs from Tusayan Ruin to Lipan Point, providing the most spacious panorama available on the South Rim. The view encompasses the distant Echo and Vermilion Cliffs on the northeastern horizon. An assortment of temples, buttes, and spires that soar from inner-canyon slopes, with names like Wotans Throne, and Vishnu, Apollo, Venus, Jupiter, and Juno Temples, are visible as well. Many were named by North Rim topographer Clarence Dutton in 1882 or by federal surveyor Françcois Matthes in 1902. Both were men with classical educations and unfettered imaginations.

Cárdenas Butte immediately below honors the Spanish conquistador Garcia Lopez de Cárdenas, who arrived somewhere near here in 1540 with a small contingent of men looking for a river route to the Sea of Cortez. Cárdenas accounted to Don Francisco Vasquez de Coronado, governor of the Province of Nueva Galicia, who, with Mexican viceroy Antonio de Mendoza, had invested 110,000 ducats (more than $2 million) to comb Mexico's northwestern frontier for riches. So far they had found nothing to fill their purses, and this side trip did not help. After three of the party failed to reach the "Rio de Tison" (Firebrand River, an early Spanish name for the Colorado), all retreated to Coronado's main army beside the Rio Grande, disgusted at what was in their eyes a barren land torn by a chasm too deep to be believed.

Hopi guides, who led Cárdenas to the highest point above the river and then neglected to show him the way down, had an entirely different perspective. This was their place of origin, a source for salt and spiritual renewal, and home to their ancestors—evidenced by extensive archaeological remains found today on Unkar Delta north of the river. Archaeologist Douglas Schwartz excavated the three-hundred-acre site in 1967-68, uncovering extensive stacked-stone rooms, ceremonial kivas, and agricultural terraces. He concluded that the fertile delta, the widest in Grand Canyon, had been occupied in periods of above-average precipitation for nearly three centuries, roughly A.D. 900-1180. As many as ten families lived here in the late eleventh century, seasonally migrating up Unkar Creek to the North Rim's Walhalla Plateau across the way.

22

DESERT VIEW

Indian Watchtower by Gunnar Widforss, circa 1933.

SITE OF THE *Watchtower,* DESIGNER MARY COLTER'S RUSTIC MASTERPIECE.

We have an unknown distance yet to run, an unknown river to explore . . . . With some eagerness and some anxiety and some misgiving we enter the canyon below.

THE "CANYON BELOW" is Grand Canyon. The trepidation was expressed by John Wesley Powell, leader of the first exploration through Grand Canyon, as he and his ill-clad, half-starved men bobbed along the fragment of river visible below.

In 1890 engineer Robert Brewster Stanton followed Powell's wake to survey a railway. Had he found the money to match his dream, we might now be gazing at rails, trains, and condominiums on the sandy flanks of the river. Stanton's scheme to develop the canyon, like countless others, failed, but his report of minerals incited a rush of prospectors who lingered into the 1920s. Reminders of them today include inner-canyon paths like Seth Tanner's trail to the river, visible to the west.

In 1928 the National Park Service, Fred Harvey Company, and Santa Fe Railroad began to develop Desert View as the eastern gateway to Grand Canyon's South Rim. Their centerpiece was the "Indian Watchtower," a steel-framed structure whose inspiration was the prehistoric stone towers built eight hundred years ago in the Four Corners region. The architect was Mary Colter, known for her Pueblo Revival building style and for meticulous attention to detail. Colter spent a year studying regional ruins before tackling the seventy-foot-high,

Mary Colter visited ruins as far away as Mesa Verde and Hovenweep (below) for inspiration before designing the Watchtower at Desert View. Hopi artist Fred Kabotie (above) was largely responsible for the murals inside the Watchtower (left).

PHOTO BY MIKE QUINN

The steel framework of the Watchtower was constructed by the bridge department of the Santa Fe Railroad to give the structure strength, but it is well concealed beneath the exterior of Kaibab Limestone. Construction was completed in 1932 and the Watchtower was dedicated (below) on 13 May 1933.

thirty-foot-wide spire in 1932. The interior—designed by Colter, Fred Kabotie, and rock art enthusiast Fred Geary—depicts historic and prehistoric Puebloan symbols and legends with petroglyphs, pictographs, and artifacts.

Kabotie called this place Kawinpi, the western boundary of Hopi ancestral lands, but "Desert View" is apt since the overlook affords a fine panorama of the parched picturesque landscape to the east. On the horizon beyond Cedar Mountain and the Little Colorado River Gorge lie the Echo Cliffs, backed by the spectral shadow of Navajo Mountain. Most of the land visible to the east is Navajo Reservation. The Painted Desert, twenty miles east, is only just visible, beyond the Echo Cliffs.

Scan the Echo Cliffs northward to where they meet the Vermilion Cliffs. This intersection marks the head of Marble Canyon, the easternmost boundary of Grand Canyon National Park. Then imagine the Colorado slicing deeply into the Marble Platform for seventy miles before emerging nearly a vertical mile beneath the point where you stand. Here the river helped erode the pastel strata of the billion-year-old Grand Canyon Supergroup into the broad valley below as it turned west to chisel through the older, more resistant rocks of the Inner Gorge.

Desert View also presents a spectacular view of the East Kaibab Monocline, a 3,000-foot-high, 150-mile-long crease in the earth's crust extending from southern Utah's Grand Staircase-Escalante National Monument to the San Francisco Peaks near Flagstaff. It forms the eastern edge of the Kaibab and Coconino Plateaus, accounting for the precipitous drop from Desert View to Cameron beside U.S. Highway 89.

BIRDS AND TREES YOU ARE LIKELY TO GLIMPSE ALONG THE SOUTH RIM OF GRAND CANYON

The pinyon pine (*Pinus edulis*) is seen at elevations below 7000 feet. The small stature of the trees belies their age; in this arid climate they grow slowly, and many are more than 200 years old. The short-needled pinyon—also spelled piñon—is prized for its edible seeds (pinyon nuts).

The ponderosa pine (*Pinus ponderosa*) is the only long-needled pine in the park. Its stature, characteristic bark, and fragrance make it easy to recognize. Look for it at elevations at or above 7000 feet. Ponderosa pines live to be about 120 years of age and reach heights in excess of 100 feet. The circular photo at left shows a detail of ponderosa bark, which smells faintly of vanilla.

The Utah juniper (*Juniperus monosperma*) is a dominant member of the South Rim forest at elevations below 7000 feet. Like the pinyon, it grows slowly. The juniper bears fragrant blue-green berries that are eaten by birds and other wildlife. Native cooks used the berries to season wild game.

If you're standing on the rim during summer months, listen for the whoosh of the **white-throated swift** (*Aeronautes saxatalis*) and **violet-green swallow** (*Tachycineta thalassina*). Swift, agile fliers, these birds dive through the air in relentless pursuit of insects and are more often heard than seen. The **raven** (*Corvus corax*) is a year-round resident of the South Rim and the bird you are most likely to see. Their large size distinguishes them from their cousin the crow. Ravens are extremely intelligent and can mimic a wide variety of animals.

SUGGESTED READING

Anderson, Michael F. *Living At The Edge: Explorers, Exploiters and Settlers of the Grand Canyon Region.* Grand Canyon Association, 1998.

Billingsley, George H., et al. *Quest for the Pillar of Gold: The Mines & Miners of the Grand Canyon.* Grand Canyon Association, 1997.

Coder, Christopher M. *An Introduction to Grand Canyon Prehistory.* Grand Canyon Association, 2000.

Grattan, Virginia L. *Mary Colter: Builder Upon the Red Earth.* Grand Canyon Natural History Association, 1992.

Houk, Rose. *An Introduction to Grand Canyon Ecology.* Grand Canyon Association, 1996.

Mangum, Richard, and Sherry Mangum. *Grand Canyon-Flagstaff Stagecoach Line: A History & Exploration Guide.* Hexagon Press, Inc., 1999.

Poling-Kempes, Lesley. *The Harvey Girls: Women Who Opened the West.* Marlowe & Company, 1989.

Price, L. Greer. *An Introduction to Grand Canyon Geology.* Grand Canyon Association, 1999.

Richmond, Al. *Cowboys, Miners, Presidents & Kings: The Story of the Grand Canyon Railway.* Northland Press, 1989.

MICHAEL F. ANDERSON is a historian of the western United States and the National Park System. A teacher and guide for Grand Canyon Field Institute, Colorado River guides, and the National Park Service, he has researched and written histories of northern Arizona and southern Utah since 1990. He is the author of *Living At The Edge: Explorers, Exploiters and Settlers of the Grand Canyon Region.* Dr. Anderson and his wife, Linda, live in Grand Canyon, Arizona, with their dogs, Cerca, Doc, and Bear.

GARY LADD is a freelance landscape photographer specializing in the wilderness interior of Grand Canyon National Park and the sandstone canyons in and around Glen Canyon National Recreation Area. His photographs have appeared in many books and periodicals, including *Life Magazine* and *Arizona Highways.* His most recent book, *Grand Canyon, Time Below the Rim,* with text by Craig Childs, showcases his photographic efforts within the rugged wilderness interior of Grand Canyon. Mr. Ladd has lived along the Colorado River in Page, Arizona, for twenty years.

All color photographs by Gary Ladd unless otherwise indicated. Color illustrations on pages 41, 65, and 71 by Wood, Ronsaville, Harlin. Black and white illustration on page 71 by Hugh Brown. All historic photographs are courtesy of the Grand Canyon National Park Museum Collection, image numbers as follows: Page 10: 4979, 9532. Page 11: 627, 9544. Page 16: 5823, 13657. Page 17: 10105, 9766. Page 18: 7448. Page 19: 16456, 637. Page 20 : 9654B, 5430. Page 21: 11414. Page 22: 9457, 9656, 9448, 5429B, 5254. Page 23: 9847. Page 24: 17446, 11818. Page 25: 4499, 11808, 49349. Page 27: 11822, 11823. Page 28: 30550, 30551, 7729 Kolb, 30476. Page 29: 22596. Page 31: 9947. Page 32: 4154. Page 34: 5426. Page 35: 9605, 18132. Page 38: 15805. Page 39: 5541, 10164, 13655. Page 40: 113[illegible] 26391. Page 41: 10988. Page 42: 16237, 17231, 17236. Page 43: 17171. Page 44: 12411. Page 45: 15823, 13656. Page 46: 12432. Page 48: 786, 5224. Page 50: 21331. Page 51: 8437, 7514, 15760, 8438. Page 52: 6115. Page 56: 5528. Page 58: 6255, 12084, 12079. Page 60: 12005, 7061. Page 61: 28093, 4903. Page 62: 5833. Page 63: 5701, 127. Page 66: 16959. Page 67: 17013, 8801, 22600. Page 68: 17010B, 8430, 5425.